Marquart's Works

VOLUME II

COMMUNISM

Edited by
Herman J. Otten

LUTHERAN NEWS, INC., New Haven, Missouri

Marquart's Works

Library of Congress Card
Lutheran News, Inc.
684 Luther Lane
New Haven, MO 63068
Published 2014
Printed in the United States of America
Lightning Source, Inc., La Vergne, TN
ISBN #978-0-9644799-6-8

TABLE OF CONTENTS

i

FOREWORD

Dr. Marquart was a beloved Professor by all the students that sat in his classes. His ability to simplify great theological concepts made him a favorite Teacher for all the students who attended the Seminary. He not only instilled in us a love for Theology, but he also showed us how it was to be applied in a pastor's daily calling.

However, these writings are not just for pastors. Even dedicated laymen will be able to grasp and learn from this great Teacher of the Church. Whenever and wherever Dr. Marquart made a presentation, you would soon see that he was eagerly sought out, not just by pastors but also by laymen. They too recognized his genius in refuting those who denied the Word of God. He was as popular with laymen as he was with pastors. Here in these volumes you will once again be able to take your place and listen to this great Teacher, as he clearly enunciates various topics from a thoroughly Lutheran perspective. Since these multiple volumes consist of the various topics that Dr. Marquart addressed over his illustrious life, you will find it hard to put these volumes down.

Having Dr. Marquart's writings in book form will once again allow this fearless Champion of the Church to speak to the issues that continue to plague the Church from one generation to the next. False doctrine continues to be rehashed and sent out with new clothes. As the Proverb goes, "there is nothing new under the sun." Dr. Marquart had the remarkable ability to dissect what the issue was, and why it was, and still is, false doctrine. Confessional Lutherans from all over the world were always eager to attend Dr. Marquart's lectures. They recognized that he was a giant among men. Anyone concerned about the welfare of the Church will want to have these volumes on their bookshelf.

It appears that the Almighty Savior of the Church, in His infinite wisdom, chooses to send out only a few Teachers of the Church. One may make a very short list of these esteemed gifts from God. Luther, Chemnitz, Gerhard, Walther, Pieper, Preus, and Marquart. Their writings stand the test of time. These men did not write for some passing fad, that is here today and then blown away by tomorrow's changing wind vane. Any pastor or layman, who has a desire and love for the Truth, will not be disappointed with these volumes. Every congregation that has a love for the Lord and His saving Gospel, would do well to purchase the writings from these Teachers of the Church. God had His good reasons for raising these men up and sending them out, and it would be wise for pastors and laymen to read, mark, learn and inwardly digest the writings of these great defenders of the Gospel.

Rev. Herman Otten is to be commended for publishing The Writings of Dr. Kurt Marquart. This may well be Rev. Otten's finest and most enduring contribution to the Church.

Rev. Ray R. Ohlendorf
Salem Lutheran Church
Taylorsville, NC
4th Sunday in Lent 2014

Acknowledgements

Well Herman,

As usual you find yourself doing what unsere beliebte Synode should have done long ago. The fact that CPH has not already published a book of Kurt's writings is an absolute travesty. It is an indictment of the politics before theology which has destroyed the orthodoxy of the LCMS. Our Savior Lutheran Church will stand by you in the worthy project. Back in the dark days when Bohlmann and his supporters were after Robert Preus we published a number of Kurt's magnificent essays on Robert's behalf. Modern Missouri has never produced another theologian comparable to him either in confessional fidelity or eloquence. We are proud and eager to take part in this belated effort. "Gottes Wort Und Luthers Lehr Vergehet Nun Und Nimmermehr."

Larry White, Pastor
Our Saviour Lutheran Church
Houston, Texas

Thanks to Luke Otten for arranging the publication of these volumes and to Naomi Finck, John Eberhart, Natalie Hoerstkamp, and Mary Zastrow for type-setting.

Thanks to Grace Otten for recognizing the importance of publishing *Marquart's Works* ever since they first began appearing in *Christian News* more than 50 years ago. Thanks to Scott Meyer, "America's confessional Lutheran" lay historian and President of the Concordia Historical Institute whose appreciation of Marquart's works and encouragement helped make the publication of these volumes possible.

PREFACE

Dr. C. F. W. Walther, first president of The Lutheran Church-Missouri Synod, has been rightly referred to as "The American Luther." As the editor of a Christian weekly for 51 years, the undersigned has reviewed thousands of books. During all these years he has published the writings of many theologians. The index at the back of Volume V of the *Christian News Encyclopedia* lists the names of hundreds of theologians whose writings have appeared in *Christian News*. Some, like Kurt Marquart, were also good friends. Yet, the editor knows of no theologian who deserves the title "The International Lutheran" more than Kurt Marquart. The editor's wife, Grace, is a graduate of Concordia College, St. Paul Minnesota and Valparaiso University. There she studied under some prominent theologians who later became professors at Concordia Seminary, St. Louis and Seminex. In 1963 Grace Otten and Kurt Marquart were *CN*'s reporters at the Fourth Assembly of the Lutheran World Federation in Helsinki, Finland. Following the LWF Assembly she and the editor's brother, Walter, who knew Marquart for 54 years, accompanied him on a twenty city lecture tour in the U.S. Grace shares the editor's evaluation of Kurt Marquart. She helped make it possible together with Luke Otten, Ruth Rethemeyer, Mary Beth Otten, Kristina Bailey and the Missourian Publishing Company, Washington, Missouri, to get *Marquart's Legacy* published in 2006 not long after his death. The 76 page *Marquart's Legacy* is available from *Christian News* for $5.00. It includes photos of Marquart and family and information about two professionally made videos showing Marquart in action.

Marquart's Legacy begins with a brief biography of Kurt Marquart. Then follows "Remembrances of a Former Seminary Roommate," the editor of *Christian News*. Next comes "The Lasting Legacy of Kurt Marquart" as expressed by many who knew him well.

The appendixes list the writings and reports of Kurt Marquart which have appeared in 44 volumes of *Christian News* (1962-2006), *A Christian Handbook on Vital Issues*, the five volumes of the *Christian News Encyclopedia, Luther Today, What Would He Do or Say?* and *Crisis in Christendom-Seminex Ablaze*. The lasting legacy of a great theologian and genius like Kurt Marquart can best be found in his works. *CN* suggested in 2006 that the Lutheran Church-Missouri Synod's Concordia Publishing House should publish *Marquart's Works*.

The questions at the end of each section are included to make *Marquart's Works* helpful for study. In an age when faith in historic Christianity is declining in all of the major denominations, *Marquart's Works* can be used to encourage and strengthen faithful Christians and begin a 21st Century Reformation and 21st Century Formula of Concord by the 500th anniversary of the Reformation in 2017.

Herman Otten
Reformation, 2014

COMMUNISM, WESTERN CIVILIZATION, AND CHRISTIANITY

A short article on a vast subject in the nature of the case calls for conclusions and generalizations which cannot be argued in detail.

Communism: Theoretical Foundation

Communism is, to use a favorite and typical phrase of Social Credit's genius, Major C. H. Douglas, "the policy of a philosophy." Any analysis of Communism which minimizes the basic ideological ingredient is bound to degenerate into illusion.

The philosophy underlying Communism is officially known as "Dialectical Materialism."

Dialectical Materialism differs from ordinary ("inconsistent," "bourgeois," i.e. non-Communist) materialism about as much as Roman Catholicism differs from the anemic would-be Christianity of Bultmann: The one is a definite, positive, comprehensive, albeit twisted dogmatism, parading as the program, "objective," "scientific" world-view and revolutionary ritually represented, enforced and propagated by a self-perpetuating well-disciplined organization with vested interests; while the other is merely a bit of arid, abstract, purely negative theorizing, from which nothing in particular—at least nothing interesting–follows, and which can therefore provide a solid basis neither for a positive system of beliefs, nor for an obligatory course of action.

Dialectics, according to Engels, is "the science of the general laws of motion, both of the external world and of human thought." This rationale makes it possible to represent social, economic, political, indeed any philosophical speculations as part and parcel of one vast and coherent "scientific" Weltanschauung. "Dialectics" is the "scientific" bridge which connects the Marxist-Leninist theories with those of materialism, from which these basic philosophical assumptions of materialism, from which those theories allegedly follow with logical necessity, and from which they therefore derive their "scientific" status.

The three basic "laws" of Dialectics are the unity of opposites, the transition of quantity into quality, and the negation of negation.

What is the aim, the point of it all? The ultimate goal is a transformed, classless society, in which a transformed mankind lives in Utopian bliss, without coercion, each receiving according to his needs, and contributing according to his ability. That will be Communism. Socialism, enforced by an admittedly harsh but necessary "dictatorship of the proletariat," (that is, a dictatorship of the General Secretary, who represents the Central Committee, which represents the Communist Party, which represents the proletariat, which represents mankind) is a preparatory stage. As the Socialist State, under the oracular guidance of the Party, succeeds in "scientifically" producing human specimens and a social organism of ever-increasing perfection, the dictatorship will gradually "wither away."

In the meantime, everyone must be subject, without question, to the said dictatorship, in order to enable it to complete its business and "wither away" the sooner!

(Note: While Stalin had decreed already in 1936 that "the complete victory of the socialist system in all spheres of the national economy is now an accomplished fact," and that "socialism, the first stage of communism, is already realized by us in the main"—Boris Souvarine, Stalin, p.603—this was never anything but propaganda fiction. Khrushchev, impressed with the utter failure of whatever "socialism" did exist, has had to use the "capitalist" device of profit-motive, in order to cope with the desperate plight of his economy!)

World Conquest

This drama, moreover, is enacted not on narrow, national stages, but in the arena of the world. World conquest is, always has been, and always will continue to be the implicit and explicit objective of Communism.

Whatever gestures Communists make toward the non-Communist world, are simply part of the strategy for gaining the objective. The strategy (always understood dialectically) may be a series of apparent reversals, but the object is always the same. Military conquest, "peaceful co-existence," nuclear test bans, labor troubles, nationalist uprisings, diplomatic treaties, cultural, scientific, etc. "exchanges," religious gatherings, and all other activities or occasions in which Communists participate, are simply tactical maneuvers within a grand strategy of world conquest. To fail to see that in Communist hands absolutely everything is regarded as a weapon for the ultimate subjugation of the world, is precisely the sort of mutton-headed and chicken-hearted outlook which guarantees Communist success. In a contest between a fairly honorable but somewhat naïve gentleman, and an unprincipled gangster, in which, moreover, the former is unaware of any conflict between them, the outcome is not hard to predict!

Since "capitalists" and "imperialists" (that is, free, civilized human beings) are not likely to submit to the "dictatorship of the proletariat" voluntarily, they must be —outwitted, deceived, tricked in every possible way, and when feasible, simply exterminated. Such a program naturally requires a strong-stomached "ethics", contemptuous of "bourgeois" squeamishness, i.e. that prissy tendency uncivilized men to abhor murder, robbery, tyranny, betrayal, and kindred manifestations of criminality.

Communist "ethics" are pure opportunism: Whatever advances the interests of the Party is good and true, everything else is evil and false. Something which is "true" today could be totally false tomorrow, which is why Soviet histories and encyclopedias are rewritten so often.

Said Lenin: "There are no morals in politics, there is only expediency." Again: "Very frequently the bourgeoisie makes the charge that we Communists deny all morality. That is one of their methods of confusing the issue... We deny all morality taken from superhuman or non-class conceptions...We say that our morality is wholly subordinated to the interests of the class struggle."

2

Religion, needless to say, is regarded as the "opiate" of the people, designed to keep the working classes enslaved.

II. Christianity, Ideology in General, and Communism in Particular

To say that Western Civilization is a historical by-product of the Incarnation is not to identify the world and the Church, human ideology and Christianity. It is merely to dramatize the truism that Western Civilization, whatever the proportions among its various ingredients, was built largely upon a foundation of Christian certainties. When these certainties were undermined by Rationalism, Materialism, Evolutionism, etc., the foundations of our civilization began to crumble. Naturally the superstructure began to collapse too, and it is the continuation of this process which is producing that unpleasant chaotic effect, which we are now beginning to take for granted under such banal journalistic labels as "the complexities of the modern world," "the problems of the space age," etc.

Is it the Church's task to "save Western Civilization"? Decidedly not! In the first place, as Toynbee remarks somewhere, "religion, once lost, cannot be whistled for, like a dog, to return at man's convenience." And God must be loved and served for His own sake, not as a means to some other end, i.e. "to save democracy". In the second place, the Church's task is spiritual and other-worldly. Roman and Calvinistic externalisms to the contrary notwithstanding, the Church is not a part of society, charged with facilitating society's efficient functioning. A few amazingly incisive sentences from an Easter editorial in a secular journal are closer to Christian truth than the volumes of "Social Gospel" nonsense produced by ecclesiastics who saw ant-hills and bee-hives through Darwinian spectacles, and became Marxists: "while creating Western Civilization, their (early Christians) minds were on something else...Our world can best be defended if it is continually renewed and corrected and occasionally defied...Like corals building the Great Barrier Reef, all these Christians created our Western civilization as the unplanned byproduct of their personal hope and labor . . . if we really wish to defend and extend it. . .we can do so only by imitating the builders whose real hope was elsewhere. . . And the glory of the Christian hope is that it is not offered to 'the world' but to living men and women for a life beyond" (*Life*, April 19, 1954).

The Church and Democracy

It is naive and theologically absurd to suppose that there is something specifically Christian about the modern "democratic" state, or that the Church's fate is bound up with the fortunes of "democracy". The Church as Church can and must exist under any form of government or social structure. In principle she is neither opposed nor committed to anything from monarchy to republic to dictatorship, provided only that government be orderly and remain within the bounds of Natural Law. Parliamentary democracy is **per se** neither more nor less acceptable, from the Christian

3

view-point, than some other arrangement. And while the Church must love all men as men, she cannot and must not love the world as world. Love of world is enmity toward God. And in this regard it makes no difference whether the world at a given time or place prefers royal scepters or ballot boxes!

In purely political matters each Christian is free, within the bounds of natural and revealed Law, to make his own choices. It is not the Church's business to prescribe or even endorse ideologies. If however, an ideology involves moral evil, the Church must warn her members against it. There can be no "separation of religion and politics" in a sense which would leave Christians free to attack and subvert, in Monday's political action, the Creed confessed on Sunday! Political action and affiliation is, potentially just as overt a denial of the Faith as, say, membership in the Masonic Lodge.

The Ancient Roman State

Communism is not simply a morally neutral ideology. This should be quite apparent. The Church has both the right and the duty to condemn Communism "as a moral evil, which violates both natural and revealed Law" (Resolution of the Queensland District, Evangelical Lutheran Church of Australia, 1962). Communism is evil not because its rulers, as individuals, happen to be atheists, but because the Communist state exists for the very purpose of enforcing an evil, consciously atheistic code of belief and behavior. In the ancient Roman state, atheism and idolatry were accidental features, not a constitutive ideology. Constantine proved that. But the Communist state is unthinkable without the Communist creed, which in turn is meaningless without its materialistic, and thus necessarily atheistic, philosophical foundation. Whatever the cynicism among the leaders, officially, at any rate, the state exists exclusively as a vehicle of the ideology. To imagine that Communism could ever, without ceasing to exist, drop its hostility to any form of theistic religion, is a careless miscalculation, is, in fact, the height of folly, as some "wishfully optimistic" German Church leaders found out to their dismay.**

Whatever temporary relief is granted to religious groups behind the Iron Curtain from time to time, is merely a dialectical maneuver, and does not in the least change the ultimate aim, which is total eradication of all anti-materialistic movements. And this means not only the destruction of the Church as an organization, but the systematic indoctrination of youth in an educational system in which the official atheistic philosophy enjoys a complete monopoly! The child belongs to the state, and the wishes of the parents do not matter whatever. Whole populations are taught to hate and loathe Christianity, as well as all representatives of non-Communist systems, and to love that monstrously immoral social cancer, Communism. Not only property rights, but human life itself is treated with contempt. Stalin murdered millions. Children are taught to betray their parents. A good citizen is only one who is prepared to murder, rob, betray, slander, or commit any other crime at the command of the Party, and to acquiesce in such actions by others. It is not merely pos-

4

itive revelation, but natural Law that is trodden underfoot.

A state whose *raison d'atre* is the repudiation of the Natural Law, and which therefore commands that which is evil and forbids that which is good, cannot be recognized as a lawful state. It is simply an embodiment of evil, a "legalized" criminality, resting entirely on brutality, not on justice. To such a state no Christian may or can render any real loyalty, in the sense of internal, conscientious obedience. Such a state can only be endured, never respected. Bishop Otto Dibelius deserves the Church's thanks and commendation for his clear vision in seeing this, and for his courage in saying it ("Demons remain demons. They will never become legitimate powers").***

Ecclesiastical Communist Propagandists

That churchmen behind the Iron Curtain cannot openly say such or similar things, is of course understandable. That some "churchmen" from those areas are shameless propagandists for various Communist causes ("coexistence," pacifism, etc.) is also understandable when one remembers that particularly since World War II the Kremlin has realized the value of Marxist propagandists attired in ecclesiastical vestments. And anyone who doubts the Communists' intention to destroy the Church also by infiltrating it from within and meanwhile using it for their own purposes, should read Walter Kolarz' Religion in the Soviet Union and Richard Solberg's God and Caesar in East Germany. (A lesson for us: Next to inner strength and integrity, rooted in a firm hold upon divine Revelation, administrative decentralization will best enable the Church to endure with dignity the living martyrdom of Communist oppression!)

What is however rather shocking is the susceptibility which Western ecclesiastics have shown toward Communist propaganda. There is the notorious case of Harry Ward, Professor at Union Theological Seminary, whose "Social Creed," prepared originally for the Methodists of the U.S.A., became the Socioeconomic bible of the Federal Council of Churches, the predecessor of the National Council of Churches of Christ in the U.S.A. Ward was an out-and-out Marxist, whose public record reveals support of dozens of Communist causes. The amount of clerical support these various causes are able to enlist, is truly astounding and disgusting. National Council leaders have even dared to advocate Red China's diplomatic recognition and admission into the U.N.O. When the top leadership of the World Council of Churches (including Chairman Franklin C. Fry, President of the "Lutheran Church in America" and of the Lutheran World Federation) unctuously rebuked the United States for its long delayed and ill-exploited defensive action in Cuba, even the theologically modernistic and politically leftish Christian Century was provoked to the point of commenting: "The present situation is that World Council officers are on record as criticizing the United States for acting openly to repel a threat to peace while they maintain silence concerning secret Soviet actions which precipitated the crisis" (Nov. 14, 1962).

Karl Barth's softness toward Communism is well-known.****

Reinhold Niebuhr, himself a modernist, makes an interesting admis-

5

sion:

There are in fact Communist sympathizers and fellow travelers in the church...It must be affirmed that there have never been many explicit Stalinists in the churches...Nevertheless there are a few and we ought to admit it...the pathetic clerical Stalinism could not have developed except against the background of a very considerable Marxist dogmatism in the "liberal" wing of the Protestant churches (quoted in *National Review,* April 9, 1960, p. 226).

The clergy have been found particularly useful in two areas of the Communist program: 1. The socio-economic destruction of Western Society by means of "Socialism" and 2. The military self-destruction of the West along "Peaceful Co-Existence" lines.

Liberal Theology
Only a very disoriented "Protestantism" can allow itself to become a tool of the Red Devil. This disorientation was achieved by the same forces that produced Marxism in the first place; Rationalism, materialism, evolutionism. Liberal "theologians," who had thrown the authority of the Bible overboard, along with all Christian dogma, became passionate addicts of a this worldly "Social Gospel," which turned out to be a sloppy, sentimental Socialism, decorated with religious slogans but devoid of any firm ethical substance which might have prevented the plunge into collectivist relativism. And it is strange that anyone should have regarded Socialism as particularly Christian. After all, from the fact that it is a virtue for me to help my neighbor and share my belongings with him, for the sake of God's love in Christ, it does not follow that it is virtuous when I am compelled to "share" my goods, or when I ask the government to compel my neighbor to share his goods with me and others!

While orthodox Christianity must unequivocally condemn the moral enormities of Communism, it will, by not obfuscating his mind with all sorts of foggy ideologies, leave the Christian citizen free to use his God given reason to arrange his political life sensibly, including a program of anti-Communism. Unlike both Romanism and Calvinism, the Lutheran Church refuses to regard itself as a social reform movement (*Augsburg Confession,* Art. XVI). Human reason is competent in the area of "civil righteousness" (Art. XVIII, 1). Positive Christianity is not necessary for good and just government. Natural Law is sufficient (It is obvious, though, that in practice some form of theism or deism is necessary to support the notion of Natural Law and to keep human reason from committing suicide by overreaching itself).

A Realistic Program of Action
"In a small town near Prague toward the end of May 1962, Communist activists from more than twenty countries met to plan the international campaign against anti-Communism." Thus reports the February 12, 1963 issue of National Review. Result? Strenuous efforts are being made to persuade the public in the West that thorough-going anti-Communists

are "extremists" who are doing more harm than good. People who for years have been propagandizing for Left-wing causes, are suddenly writing manuals on "how to fight Communism" (Herman F. Reissig's "How To Combat Communism," for example). The Communists and their fellow travelers are obviously frightened by the intensity and effectiveness of a growing "grassroots" anti-Communism, and are trying to scatter and misdirect this energy. This new anti-anti-Communism is the more dangerous, the more sincere and well-meaning its purveyors. After all, as Major Douglas observed once, "it is not arsenic in a bottle, and labeled, that is dangerous, but arsenic in good soup"!

"Just Preach the Gospel"

Unfortunately also Lutheran clergyman-correspondent Lambert Brose's book How To Fight Communism Today (Concordia 1962) is highly unsatisfactory precisely in this regard. One notices, side by side with some very good and valuable points, certain serious deficiencies: A tendency to think in clichés, namely those popularized by modern collectivism; and aversion to cutting but necessary distinctions, traceable, one feels, to the reigning amoral, relativistic journalism's practice of distributing blame as evenly as possible, according to the egalitarian maxim that quod licet *Jovi, licet bovi*; the ominous silence about the use of political and military power, (except for a rejection of the principle of unilateral disarmament); the preoccupation instead with such collectivist obsessions— all assigned totally unrealistic, disproportionate remedial powers—as race integration, gigantic give-away programs("foreign aid") anti-colonialism, and of course the dreadful "far Right" extremists; the overall lack of clear ideological vision; and last, but not least, the incredibly naive conception, bordering on magic, of the place of Christian faith in the struggle against Communism. It is rather superficial to meet every problem with the assertion that it would be solved if non-Christians became Christians and Christians became better Christians. That is not a solution, but a restatement of the problem. Of course it would be nice if all criminals would become saints. But they don't. What's more, no "scientific psychology," no bureau of even the most ponderous of modern welfare states will ever be able to work such a miracle! Some things even committees and huge, inflationary appropriations cannot accomplish. Until this situation improves out of existence, we shall have to endure such distasteful nuisances as prisons, police forces, etc., in order to protect to some extent the civilized community. And if this is true on the local and national level, why should it be otherwise on the international level?

Communism must be fought both as an ideology and as a political power. (It is suicidal mania for certain Western sentimentalists to suggest in effect that since "Communism is an ideology"— a dangerous half-truth all–that is necessary is that we drop our weapons and read some Sunday School rhymes to Mr. Khrushchev!) Individuals must find or found, and then support, publications and organizations able and willing to inflict telling blows upon the enemy.

7

Study the Issues

The ideological struggle requires informed, alert citizens, who not only know the relevant facts, but are also able to understand their significance. Bright youngsters should learn Communist theory sufficiently to be able to ask embarrassing questions at union meetings or in informal discussions with Marxists or people infected by Marxism:(For example: "Why, if 'capitalist oppression' must be overthrown by violent revolution, must the 'dictatorship of the proletariat' be allowed to 'wither away' of its own accord, by gradual evolution?" or: "If Dialectics is so basic to nature and human history, why should it simply stop when Communism is attained? Will not new opposites arise, and will not the Communist negation in turn bring about its own negation? If not, why not?")

It is vital to read truly informative material. Good books on practically all aspects of Communism can be secured through the Heritage Bookshop (Australian League of Rights), Box 105-2J, G.P.O., Melbourne. Easily the sanest and best American contribution to the defense of Western Civilization against the new barbarians is the fortnightly journal *National Review*. 150 East 35th St., New York 16, N.Y., U.S.A. (10 dollars per annum).

And here is a bait which, if swallowed, will introduce the reader to a surprisingly vast and fascinating body of literature: "Why philosophic communists haven't flocked to Douglas, and why canting levelers haven't flocked to Gesell is a mystery or would be if one failed to allow for the non-existence of philosophic communists, or for the lack of any real reasoning or intelligence among levelers (dominated by hate and envy and deficient in the greater part of the sensitive and perceptive gamut)" (Ezra Pound, *Impact*. Chicago. Henry Regnery Company,1960, p. 243).

Having studied the situation carefully, the interested citizen will find that there is astonishingly much that he as an individual can do. Lectures, study-clubs, letters to the editor can be employed to spread the truth about Communism. Informed workers could combine to oust pro-Communist trade-union officials, or at least to expose them. (The extent which Australian Communists are able to infiltrate and influence important sectors of public life is truly appalling. The July 1962 number of the Toowoomba R.S.L's *Official Journal*, reports in a well-documented article: "Communists still have Australia by the throat. In spite of efforts by a number of Unions, Communist infiltration in the Trade Unions continues, to the extent that vast damage can be done to National Defense in the event of any emergency.")

The Intelligent Anti-Communist

The intelligent anti-Communist must be aware of two tendencies in the politics of the Western nations: (1) A collectivist, socialist tendency, which seeks to centralize government, and to put more and more areas of the citizens' lives under the direct or indirect control of an expanding bureaucracy, (2) an insistence on constitutional, limited, de-centralized government, with as much emphasis as possible placed on personal liberty, individual responsibility and in initiative, the inviolability of basic

8

rights, including property rights, and so on.

Practically every political election in the British Commonwealth or the U.S.A. offers the voter an opportunity to choose between (1) and (2), even if, unfortunately, the choice is often between different degrees of (1). By defeating (1) as much as possible, wherever and whenever it may appear, the voter is effectively fighting the vanguard of Communism. That this is how the Communists themselves understand the situation, of that there can be no doubt. The late William Z. Foster, leader of American Communism, was advised by Stalin himself to the effect that the American people would not accept Communism at once and that this system must therefore be imposed gradually and imperceptibly, i.e. by way of "a consistent but gradual increase in local and federal public ownership projects" which will "result in a final acceptance of complete government ownership and operation...Every new local or federal public ownership project is an added nail in the coffin that will finally contain capitalism... the average left-wing American liberal, who would be insulted at being called a Socialist or a Communist, would enthusiastically use all of his influence to bring about more public ownership operations in the field of natural resources, transportation and other commercial lines. That is the way we must enlist the left-wing liberals in all walks of life, not only in the United States, but in all Latin America as well" (quoted in Christian Economics. April 17, 1962). And Mao Tse-Tung's bellicose little pamphlet "on People's Democratic Dictatorship" contains this revealing paragraph: "The Communist Parties and the progressive parties and groups in Britain and America are at this moment campaigning for the establishment of trade and even diplomatic relations with us. This is goodwill. This is aid. This cannot be spoken of in the same breath as the actions of the bourgeoisie in these countries."

The struggle is likely to be protracted, complicated, and intense. Perhaps, by God's undeserved mercy and protection, we shall be delivered. Christian citizens will commend themselves, their country, and their Sovereign to Him Who alone is their Refuge and Strength!

NOTES

*Quoted in Paul Blanshard, *Communism, Democracy, and Catholic Power* (Boston: The Beacon Press, 1952), pp. 183-184.

**Richard W. Solberg, *God and Caesar in East Germany* (New York: The Macmillan Company, 1961), p. 179.

***lbid., p. 289.

****Ibid., pp. 278 ff.

Christian News, August 26, 1963

1. What philosophy underlies Communism? ____.
2. What is the implicit and explicit objective of Communism? ____.
3. Communist "ethics" are pure ____.
4. Religion is regarded as the ____ people.
5. Western Civilization was largely built upon ____.
6. The Church's task is ____ .

7. Is the Church's fate bound up with the fortunes of democracy? ___.
8. Is it the Church's business to endorse ideologies? ____.
9. Does the Church have the right to condemn Communism? ____.
10. In what sense can there be no separation of religion and politics?
    ____.

11. According to Communism, the child belongs to the ____ .
12. What kind of state cannot be regarded as a lawful state? ____.
13. What did Harry Ward of Union Seminary in New York promote?
    ____.

14. What was Karl Barth's attitude toward Communism? ____.
15. The Lutheran Church refuses to regard itself as ____.
16. The intelligent anti-Communist must be aware of ____.

THE CHRISTIAN CHURCH
AND COMMUNISM

I. Theoretical Incompatibility

The ecclesiastical branch of the Leftist pseudo-intelligentsia assiduously cultivates the superstition that Christianity and communism can and ought to find certain limited areas of "co-operation." Since, (1) Communism is nothing but a kind of Christian idealism gone sour and (2) the two systems therefore have certain common goals or objectives for the effective attainment of which the misguided communists need the corrective "witness" of their Christian brethren!

Let the following two quotes suffice as illustrations:

A Christian's Handbook on Communism, a recent (1962) publication of the National Council of Churches of Christ in the U.S.A., states, in its conclusions:

"The great appeal of communism to people of high ideals is that it proposes a prompt and vigorous remedy for some of the worst evils in modern society. Christians in many countries have felt the force of that appeal. They have asked themselves, 'Can this movement be evil when its followers fight against social evils?' Should not Christians, while keeping their eyes open, co-operate with communism, at least to a limited degree, as long as it continues to work toward real Christian objectives.

"You must answer such questions for yourself."

In *Communism and the Christian Faith* published by the LCMS's Concordia Publishing House, Robert Scharlemann solemnly instructs us as follows:

"In calling communism a Christian heresy (the word should perhaps be put into quotation marks) we mean first that some of its basic motifs are derived, directly or indirectly, from Biblical religion. Two convictions in particular are shared by Biblical Christianity and communism.

"The first is a concern for history. It is the conviction that persons, events, and the course of happenings in this world have an importance of their own...

"The second common concern is the passion for social justice."

Really! But how sophisticated—isn't it!—to evoke a sense of solidarity among Christians with a term like "Christian heresy," with or without quotation marks!

Egg-Headed Alienation from Reality

If one meant to indulge in bitter irony, one might be excused for saying that communism has a "concern for history." After all, horse thieves have a "concern" for horses, bank-robbers and counterfeiters for money, abortionists for medical science, etc. but to offer such statements as sober observations is to reveal that perverse, egg-headed alienation from reality which has aided and abetted the communist enterprise for lo, these many years!

11

No one who is at all familiar with the communist concept of truth (whatever helps the Party is true), with the utter contempt for historical facts which characterizes all the oft-revised encyclopedia and history books of the Soviet Union, and with the blatant, systematic lies spread throughout the world day in and day out by this most brazen, most colossal, and most cynical propaganda machine of all time, can possibly speak of a communist "concern for history." And people not familiar with the situation shouldn't write about it!

And what of communism's alleged "passion for social justice"? How can any self-respecting person on this side of the Iron Curtain write such rubbish? Of course "social justice" is used as bait for underlings, dupes, and suckers. But can anyone seriously imagine Stalin or Khrushchev sincerely contemplating ways and means of helping their terrorist "government" to "wither away," as the theory puts it? How can anyone be so totally lacking in an elementary sense of honor as to insult the memories of millions of past and present victims—many of them martyrs for the Faith—of the communist butchers and mass-murderers, suggesting that these unparalleled barbarities somehow bespeak a "passion for social justice"? Are bloodbaths "social justice" merely because they are perpetrated in the name of some alleged ultimate utopia, whose attainment depends on the physical extermination of whole classes of mankind? Was Hitler's "liquidation" of millions of Jews ever understood to issue from a sincere but misguided "passion for social justice"? Why this lunatic preference for communist barbarity over Nazi barbarity? Do successful criminals, operating on a vast, global scale, merit greater leniency than unsuccessful, merely regional ones?

But, it may be argued, communist theory may be ever so unrealistic, and its organizational representatives ever so hypocritical in its application; still, is not the basic vision, the ideal, "inherited from the Judeo-Christian tradition?"

A Return to Pagan Mythologies

Karl Marx was born in Prussia in 1818 of Jewish parents. His father, a lawyer, professed acceptance of Christianity after a government edict had made it difficult for non-Christians to hold public office. Karl became antagonistic to all religion, including Judaism. From the elements of a rigorous atheism and materialism, Hegelian dialectics, and Darwinian evolutionism, Marx, at the University of Berlin, shaped his militant ideology of class warfare. Are these ingredients of a "Judeo-Christian" nature? Are they not rather a deliberate rejection of two millennia of Christian civilization, and a return to pagan mythologies? In point of fact Marx consciously sides with pagan antiquity against Christiantiy.[1]

Marx wrote: "The democratic concept of men is false because it is Christian. The democratic concept holds that each man is a sovereign being. This is the illusion, dream, and postulate of Christainty."[2] Are these "Judeo-Christian" sentiments?

It is simply not true that any sort of utopian scheme necessarily procedes from Christian ideals. Consider the following typically Marxist

12

point of view, intent upon "fashioning the State with a view to the greatest happiness, not of any particular class, but of the whole".

"Shall we try to find a common basis by asking of ourselves what ought to be the chief aim of the legislator in making laws and in the organization of a State,—what is the greatest good, and what is the greatest evil...?
...Can there be any greater evil than discord and distraction and plurality where unity ought to reign? Or any greater good than the bond of unity? There cannot. And there is unity where there is community of pleasures and pains—where all the citizens are glad or grieved on the same occasions of joy and sorrow? No doubt. Yes, and where there is no common but only private feeling a State is disorganized—when you have one half of the world triumphing and the other plunged in grief at the same events happening to the city for the citizens certainly. Such differences commonly originate in a disagreement about the use of the terms 'mine' and 'not mine,' 'his' and 'not his'. Exactly so. And is not that the best-ordered state in which the greatest number of persons apply the terms 'mine' and 'not mine' in the same way to the same thing? Quite true, or that again which most nearly approves to the condition of the individual –as in the body, when but a finger of one of us is hurt, the whole frame...feels the hurt and sympathizes all together with the part affected...very true, he replied, and I agree with you that in the best-ordered State there is the nearest approach to this common feeling which you describe.

"Then when any one of the citizens experiences any good or evil, the whole State will make his case their own, and will either rejoice or sorrow with him? Yes, he said, that is what will happen in a well-ordered State."

Platonic Paganism Inspires Collectivist Totalitarianism

Is this a "Judeo-Christian" dream? Hardly. It is that of the ancient pagan, Plato, as expressed in "The Republic"! It is not Christianity, with its realistic doctrine of original sin, but optimistic, Platonic Paganism, which inspires collectivist totalitarianism, and its shallow, Pavlov-Lysenko notions of human nature.

And if communism appeals, and intends to appeal, to certain ethical-idealistic leftovers from Christianity, minus the dogmatic foundation—which, incidentally, disappeared for most of our contemporaries in the same bottomless abyss out of which communism arose—then from the Christian stand-point this is an added reason for an unqualified condemnation. The Greek work "anti", used figuratively, means "in place of", or "instead of." Not crude contradictions but subtle substitutions are the essence of Anti-Christ! The communist vision of a paradise without God is anti-Christian precisely in the measure in which it resembles the Christian conception! And it need not surprise any Christian when all efforts to implement this "paradisiacal" vision in terms of concrete, historical realities, succeed only in producing progressively the closest approximations to hell which have been inflicted upon this earth!

In 1942 a communist propaganda journal, *The Protestant*, run by leftist American clergymen, stated:

"It is clear that Marx's attack on religion is primarily an attack on su-

13

pernaturalism or otherworldliness which is indifferent to human needs and development. His views are quite in harmony with humanistic and naturalistic philosophies of religion. They are altogether acceptable to those who, with Matthew Arnold, find the essence of religion to be 'morality touched by emotion.'...Marxism and democracy and a liberal religious faith are as one."[3]

It is quite true that a denatured, apostate "Christianity" (or "liberal religious faith") has much in common with Marxism, for they are both products of the same historical forces. But genuine Christian faith can have no sentimental illusions about having anything "in common" with a brutal, criminal policy based on an atheistic, materialistic philosophy!

II. The Oppression of the Church Behind the Iron Curtain

It is saddening, indeed nauseating, to contemplate the spectacle of Western delegations, also ecclesiastical delegations, returning from brief chaperoned expeditions behind the Iron Curtain, and then disgorging upon a helpless public such propaganda tidbits as that, while there are certain difficulties, religious liberty can and does exist under communism! Equally revolting are the attempts of unctuous, Sadducean church politicians to portray an attitude of uncritical, stupid credulity toward communist utterances and actions as the supreme duty of "Christian love"! But there is a difference between the "Foolishness of the Gospel" and the foolishness of the unprincipled organization. Men who appear to be so influential in ecclesiastical affairs nowadays! And charity "rejoiceth not in iniquity, but rejoiceth in the truth" (I Cor. 13:6).

It has been suggested, and very wisely, that anyone who wishes to understand the situation behind the Iron Curtain, would do far better to repair to his local public library for a fortnight, than to spend the same two weeks touring China or the Soviet Union!

Communist theory is and always has been dedicated to the total destruction of the Christian Church and all other religious bodies. Apparent toleration can be only a temporary tactical maneuver.

Suppression and exploitation of churches have been the alternating, and even the simultaneous policies of communist states. All church organizations are to be destroyed, but if in the meantime, they can profitably be used for communist purposes, so much the better. For detailed documentation I would suggest such books as Walter Kolarz' *Religion in the Soviet Union* and Richard Solberg's *God and Caesar in East Germany*. Further materials are suggested in the following paragraphs from a critical review of a National Council of Churches (U.S.A.) pamphlet on communism:

A Barefaced Lie

"This entire chapter is so thoroughly dishonest that a paragraph by paragraph refutation and exposure would seem in order were it not for lack of space. Consider the second paragraph:

14

"Many things appear to indicate that communist governments give full religious freedom to Christians. Practically all of the communist countries guarantee freedom of worship in their constitutions. Seldom today are Christians being persecuted directly for their religious faith. Churchmen are tried, but it is for crimes that they are said to have committed, not for the faith they hold.

"Note the double qualification—'seldom' and 'today'. And, of course, it is notorious that church leaders by the thousands have been persecuted in the past and usually for such crime as 'espionage', 'currency speculation,' and 'anti-state activity.' In China alone the Canadian Catholic nuns who were tormented and mistreated in Shanghai were charged with 'murdering' hundreds of babies left in their care—not for practicing their religion and seeking to save Chinese girl babies abandoned in ditches and alleys.

"On page 57 under 'The Church in China' we learn that 'although there is no positive evidence that any church leader has been put to death, communism has removed from office leaders critical of the communist regime so that the church in China is a thoroughly captive church.' This statement is a barefaced lie and was written by either a writer, or writers who, made no effort whatever to check the facts and dishonestly made an unsupportable assertion hoping it would pass unnoticed.

"*The Red Book of the Persecuted Church* by John Falter, Newman Press, 1957, quotes that China Missionary Bulletin, 1948, as giving the names and details of 'more than 100 priests who were put to death often under the most inhuman conditions' between 1947 and 1948 alone. *The Systematic Destruction of the Catholic Church in China* by Thomas Bauer, *World Horizons Reports*, New York, 1954, states: 'In the eight years from 1946 to 1954 a total of 166 members of the secular clergy and religious orders, both male and female, Chinese and foreign, have been executed by the government or had died of mistreatment in prison at the hands of their jailers'. This report then appends the names and details of their deaths at the hands of the communists.

"In addition there are a dozen or more books by Edward Hunter, Liu Shaw-tong, Rigney, Winance, Robert W. Greene, Dr. Paul K.T. Sih, Mark Tennien, De Jaegher, and Chow Ching-wen, to mention only a few, which cite cases and name names of Christian clergy and medical missionaries tortured and murdered by the Chinese Reds.

"Greta Palmer's 'God's Underground in Asia' (Appleton-Century-Crofts, 1953) is devoted entirely to recounting the murders of religious workers Catholic and Protestant, by the Chinese communists and the murderous persecution of the church in China. Hunter's *Black Book on Red China* (Bookmailer, New York, 1958) devotes a whole chapter to 'Martyred Religion'. Olin Stockwell's 'with God in Red China' (Harper Brothers, New York, 1953) is subtitled 'What is Happening to Christians in China.' Not one, strange as it may seem, is mentioned in the N.C.C.C.'s *Christians' Handbook on Communism'*.

"Last but not least in importance, is the testimony by several Protestant Chinese clergymen before the House Committee on Un-American

15

Activities in March, 1959, and released as 'Communist Persecution of Churches in Red China and Korea'. The N.C.C.C. handbook does not mention it." [5]

Execution and Deportation of the Clergy

When I was in London a few weeks ago, I obtained from a very well informed Russian Orthodox priest, Father G. Sheremtieff, a copy of a letter which he had sent to the Archbishop of Canterbury, Dr. Ramsay. The letter details the three phases of persecution suffered by the Russian Orthodox Church under communism. I quote:

"The first consisted in the physical destruction of the Church with intensified anti-Christian propaganda, execution and deportation of the clergy and destruction of churches—The first victims were the very well-known Metropolitan of Kiev,Vladimir, and the Metropolitan of Petrograd, Benjamin. After that, most of the Metropolitans and bishops followed and filled the terrible death list.

"This physical destruction of the Church continues till now. The Metropolitan Nicholas Krutizky was poisoned in hospital in Krushchev's time.

"The next step of the anti-Christian authority was the creation of the 'living' church...

"The present Patriarch of Moscow, Alexei Simansky, being bishop at that time, went over to the 'living' church (which cooperated with the Reds, K.M.); but as it had no success, he returned 'repentant' to Patriarch Tikhon...

"The Patriarch Tikhon, seeing that all his Metropolitans were deported and executed, proclaimed to all believers: 'I call you, beloved children of the Orthodox Church, to follow me in suffering and tortures.'

"After that the Patriarch Tikhon proclaimed the anathema (excommunication) against the communist authorities and against all who follow and work with them...

Bolshevik Doctors Gave Him an Injection

"Soon after the Patriarch, being arrested and ill-treated, fell ill and was taken to hospital. Once in the absence of the head doctor of this hospital, a party of Bolshevik doctors came officially to verify the state of health of the Patriarch. They gave him an injection and departed when the head-doctor came back, all his efforts to save the Patriarch were in vain and he died...

"The next phase was the seizure of the Church administration and the creation of new bishops devoted to the communist party. It was done in this way:

"All the Metropolitans who could succeed Patriarch Tikhon were deported or murdered. The communist tries to find a traitor among the High Clergy, who would consent to introduce the political police into the Church administration, but could not find one. At least they dealt with Metropolitan Sergius, who also refused to recognize them. But after three years of imprisonment, he submitted not only for himself but also for the whole Church. He wrote a declaration in which he recognized the communist government as a legal one; further he proclaimed that there had never been any persecutions absent the Church; that all the executed bishops were not martyrs for Faith but political offenders, who were rightly punished; that every success of the communist party was also his and his Church's 'success'. After that, he introduced members of the political police into the Church administration...

A Communist Tool

"From that moment, when the political police was introduced into the church governing board, it became a tool in the hands of the godless communist international organization, which is fighting against the Church of Christ.

"After the 'Declaration' the Church became divided. The part, which did not recognize the political actions of Sergius, was called the 'Tikhon Church'. And the Sergius Church received the nickname of 'fall down and worship me' (Matt. 4.9), given by the simple people.

"The Tikhon Church was strongly persecuted; but some bishops went into hiding places and consecrated new priests, who travelled on foot, dressed as peasants and officiated, christened, and married people at night in unknown sheds. When caught, they were executed...

"The soviet church calls itself the 'Patriarchal' Church but we cannot accept this title for three reasons:

"1. The soviet church working under the communist party is under the interdiction of Patriarch Tikhon, and therefore cannot represent a Patriarchal Church.

"2. The election of Patriarch Alexei Simanksy was as non-canonical as the election of Metropolitan Sergius. He was elected by bishops, whose fidelity to the communist authorities was quite certain and verified by the political police. Therefore, we cannot recognize him as a real Patriarch.

"3. The title 'Patriarchal Church' is a fraud and a lie, which was given to deceive and attract credulous people by this historical name.

"Those who now visit the U.S.S.R. remark that the churches in Moscow are overfull with believers. This is quite comprehensible: in the old Moscow there were more than two thousand churches; and now only about twenty are opened for worship and the population has increased in number (750,000 before the revolution, and about 7,000,000 now)...

"We do not accuse or criticize some lower bishops and the clergy in the U.S.S.R., for they are living under pressure and terror; they have no possibility to act otherwise. God knows what we should have done in their place..."

Secret Police Controls Religious Activities

At the hearing of the United States internal Security Subcommittee, Peter Deriabian, a former major of the Soviet Secret Police, the highest-ranking one ever to seek asylum in the West, testified under oath that all public religious activities in the Soviet Union are under the control of

Georgi Karpov, major general of the secret police. "In each province Karpov's officers are in every city where they work with KVD, taking care of all church activities." Karpov, appointed by Stalin himself, served in a twofold capacity: (1) destroying the churches for the Communist Party and (2) administering the churches and exploiting them for communist purposes! On April 12, 1956, at a hearing of the same committee, Yuri Rastvorov, a Soviet police agent for eleven years, who operated in the ecclesiastical area, testified that all churches are totally controlled by the secret police in the Soviet Union. He explained that a few seminaries had been opened, to which the secret police sent counter-intelligence officers, who later became bishops and leaders in many churches of the U.S.S.R!

One of the Russian Orthodox leaders identified by Deriabian, as a secret police agent of long standing was Metropolitan Nikolai, then second in command in the Russian Orthodox Church of the U.S.S.R.! "He became part of Premier Stalin's personal entourage, and began a subtle campaign to 'deify' the dictator," said the *New York Herald Tribune* in an obituary following his death on December 13, 1961. And it was this Metropolitan Nikolai, who handled relations with overseas churches and their delegations!

An Arm of the Soviet Embassy

Nikolai's place was taken by Archbishop Nikodim, who led the Soviet delegation to the World Council of Churches Assembly in New Delhi. Although the Associated Press of America did not report this, it is a fact that at New Delhi the Moscow delegation acted as an arm of the Soviet Embassy.[6] Nikodim arrived at meetings in the Soviet Embassy limousine. The Russian delegation invited the other delegates to Travencore Hall, a part of the Soviet Embassy, for a Sunday afternoon reception, at which a propaganda film was screened! Nikodim and four others of his delegation were elected to the Central Committee of the World Council at New Delhi! What a disgrace to the Christian name!

A former official of the Red Chinese Foreign Office relates the following experiences from his student days in Moscow:

"In a desperate attempt to cling to my faith I visited various churches in Moscow. In some of these, the congregations were large. At least I thought so but then I had been used to small numbers. What impressed me most was the absence of young men in these churches. The congregations were mostly of old people. I listened attentively to all that was said and although my Russian was not the best, I could follow most of what went on. I expected to hear the people exhorted to follow Christ as my father used to do but instead they were urged to be loyal to the Government and carry out its directions. I always came away disappointed."[7]

Penalties Increasing

Is the shoe-thumping, filthy-mouthed Khrushchev more "moderate" and "reasonable" toward religion? A revised law, "Amendments to the Criminal Code of the Russian Soviet Federated Socialist Republic," adopted on July 25, 962, by the Supreme Soviet of said "Republic" indi-

18

cates that penalties and restrictions are actually increasing. According to the November, 1962, number of *Sovetskaya Iustitsia* (Soviet Jurisprudence), the official organ of the Ministry of Justice and of the Supreme Court of the RSFSR, the new law "fixes the responsibility, the guilt, and the punishment for drawing into a religious group an underage, minor child. The...guilty ones may be the parents as well as any other person who invites any under aged, minor child to attend a religious function. The punishment for the violation of the first part of Statute 227 of the Criminal code of the RSFSR is five years imprisonment or five years of exile."[8]

The same tight control over the churches is maintained in the outlying provinces of the Soviet Empire. On December 9, 1959, the *New York Times* reported on a speech in the United Nations, in which Janos Peter, First Deputy Foreign Minister of communist Hungary, defended the brutal suppression of the heroic revolution of 1956. Who was Janos Peter? He had appeared in clerical garb at the World Council of Churches Assembly at Evanston, U.S.A., in 1954, as a bishop, representing the Hungarian Reformed Church, in which capacity he had given to the press propaganda statements regarding freedom of religion under communism, etc.! The head of the Hungarian Reformed Church is Albert Bereczky, a former member of the communist underground ,who, incidentally, was elected to the Central Committee of the World Council of Churches in 1955!

In Czechoslovakia there is the notorious Joseph L. Hromadka, another "ecumenical" figure, who has been identified as a communist tool in *Communist Penetration Into Australian Churches* by former Czech communist writer V.L. Borin, published by the Victorian League of Rights. And Dr. Michael Zibrin, a former member of the Parliament in Prague, and former Superintendent of the Lutheran Church in Slovakia, informs us that the present head of that church, Chabada, is a communist agent. He also writes:[9]

"A reorganization of the Lutheran Church had started—and what a reorganization! Faithful pastors were in every case imprisoned and ousted, and their offices were given to women with Communist Party cards. They had practically no schooling, no fitness for their work, no love of God, in fact no religion at all. Their manners and behavior made a mockery of the church!"

The LWF Admits Communist Controlled Churches

At the Fourth Assembly of the Lutheran World Federation in Helsinki this year, the Latvian Lutheran Church in Exile distributed a pamphlet titled "The Lutheran Church of Latvia in Chains," which details the true state of affairs in that unhappy Baltic country. From this pamphlet it transpires, for example, that "Archbishop" G. Turs, who represented the Latvian Church at Helsinki, is not only a communist propagandist, but had been dismissed from the pastorate in Bauska for moral reasons! Despite the protests of the Estonian and Latvian Churches in Exile, the Soviet controlled churches of these Baltic countries were admitted into the membership of the Lutheran World Federation at Helsinki. In the case of these two churches the members of the Helsinki Assembly were insulted with the following disgusting "explanation" by the Executive Committee of the Federation:

"After receiving sufficient information that the Estonian (Latvian) Church enjoyed autonomy in matters of theological training and the appointment of pastors and was financially self-supporting, it was felt that there was nothing in the church's constitution which would prevent its being accepted into membership in the LWF. In this connection, the Executive Committee has examined in great detail the objections which the Estonian (Latvian) Church (in Exile) has raised against the proposed membership in the LWF of the Lutheran Church of Estonia. While fully appreciating the difficulties that will arise for the Estonian (Latvian) Church (in Exile), it is evident that the church in the Estonian (Latvian) homeland cannot be properly represented by the church in exile, its wish to be represented in its own right must therefore be considered justifiable."

Border on Lunacy

The assumption that a communist-controlled church apparatus can be "autonomous" and capable of genuinely representing the "church in the ...homeland" borders in lunacy. It represents either a colossally irresponsible ignorance of the truth, or a cynical disregard for it. The "ecumenical" craving to hobnob with miserable communist creatures forced to pose as ecclesiastical dignitaries is simply vile! The Latvian pamphlet correctly states:

HOW TO HELP THE CHURCH IN CHAINS

"1. The Free Churches of the West are trying 'at all costs' to obtain contacts with the churches in the Soviet Union, 'no matter what they are like', because even the church in Chains is regarded as Christian...

"But they forget the differences which exist between the Church in chains **today** and the Church at the **dawn of Christianity**...they forget that it is not the Christian church in the Soviet Union which offers this contact freely, but that it is constrained to do so by the communist ideology of the State of **political** reasons....

"In the present situations:

"(a) There is no practical opportunity of giving positive help—not with Christian literature (all imported Bibles and theological literature are confiscated), nor with economic aid (remember the tragic occurrence concerning the Lutheran Bishop of Hungary, Ordass!)

"But in addition:

"(b) Such 'at all costs' contact with the Church we would help is worse than useless, because such contact reaches only the church Administration which is in the grip of the Soviet State. The truly religious Christians there are still isolated. Moreover, when the ordinary Christian believer in the Soviet Union witnesses these meetings between foreign Christian visitor and communist leaders conducted in friendly fashion, he despairs. As the prophet, Elias said: 'Lord, there is no one who has not bowed down before Baal.'"

Mao the Real Christ

As regards the situation in China, we have the interesting testimony of a former Chinese Foreign Office employee, as given in an interview with Dr. W. G. Goddard:

"Thus, while Mao was to be regarded as the real ancestor of the family, he was also to be real Christ, the true Buddha, and Allah. The stream was not dammed, it was just diverted, redirected...

"In the earlier stages of communist control, there was an attempt to suppress all religious observance. In 1950 and the following year this campaign was most intense. They were dark years indeed. But I don't think Mao had much to do with this as he was too busy establishing the regime. When he did have time to look into things, he realized that suppression was not the answer. He knew that the spiritual potential of the people was the one force that could not be destroyed. So he decided to use this spiritual potential, to redirect it into his own channels...

"He began by issuing orders to Sheng Ko, Ho Sheng, and other anti-religious propagandists to cease their campaigns. That was the first step. Then, in 1952, he convened a conference of selected revisionists to draw up plans for canalizing this religious instinct of the people...The Christian Gospels were rewritten and the Buddhist Sutras and the Koran translated with a Marxian slant...

"A commentary was appended to these new translations. Jesus was set forth as a carpenter engaged in a bitter struggle with the rich men of Nazareth. His father Joseph had been an ardent communist. Jesus had won over a small group of fishermen and several others in key positions, including a banker's clerk, Matthew. The Jewish capitalists had Jesus executed but before he died he told his followers that communism would ultimately win and in the meantime they must share everything, including their wages. This small group became the first Christian Church which was a communist society, but the bankers soon brought over most of the members with the result that the Church became the tool of the rich. Communism in China is a return to what Jesus taught and it aims at restoring primitive Christianity...

"Mao had not yet finished his redirection. He selected key men in each religious section to push ahead his plan. He won over Pi Shu-shih, a well-known Catholic in Mukden, and several other Catholic priests including Chen Yuen-tsai, of Kweiyong ,Tong Ling-tson, of Kumming, and Chao Yong-ming, of Shansi. Among the Buddhists, he selected Chen Ming-shu, Chia-t'so, and Chao Pu-chu. These were all officials of the party. After some threatening he secured the cooperation of such leading Moslems as Ma Yu-huai and Yu Su-fu."

"What of the Protestant bodies? The Presbyterians for instance? Your father had been a Presbyterian pastor."

"Possibly you know that the Presbyterians joined with other groups to form the Church of Christ in China. The Moderator of this Church of Christ is Rev. Y.T. Wu, who had been the executive Secretary of the Y.M.C.A. He had, for some time, worked closely with Peking, and was associated with the establishment of the Three Self Patriotic Movement...I do know and everybody in China who reads the newspapers knows the pledge given by every bishop and others with the oversight of churches. I did hear that Y.T. Wu was responsible for the exact wording of it... 'I pledge to guide the people under my care along the road to socialism under the direction of the Communist Party.'" [10]

China and the Social Gospel

Anglican missionary Paul B. Denlinger reports:

"Before and after the communists took over, there were two important personalities in the Chinese religious world. One was Chao Tse-Ch'en (T.C. Chao), Dean of the School of Religions at Yenching University, a united Protestant school on the outskirts of Peking. This man was one of the vice-president of the World Council of Churches at the time of the communist takeover, but he resigned this post at the insistence of the communists. He was a very active leader in the ecumenical movement in China...

"The second man was Wu Yao-tsung (Y.T. Wu. K. M.)...He had had a very good education—I believe at Union Theological Seminary in New York. Both of these men represented the point of view that distrusts imperialism, distrusts capitalism, and is interested in a kind of socialism which is dignified religiously by calling it the Social Gospel. Both men lack roots in any particular Christian denomination...both men were financed quite well by the ecumenical movement and were interested in the type of Christianity which deals only with a social mission, or in socialism. These men eased the transition when the communists took over by telling their fellow Chinese Christians that 'Christianity must be prepared to adapt so that it can live in any political situation.'...

"We began to get sermons in our local church about Jesus Christ being a great revolutionary and how he was interested in changing the world. Eventually, we got out-and-out communism, not even cloaked in the Social Gospel. It got to be so hard to take that we could hardly say our prayers...

"The hierarchy of the church in China was completely discredited in the eyes of Chinese Christians...Any priest whom the people respected was under constant pressure for the regime, and under attack and criticism from the hierarchy of his own church. Seeing this, the lay Christians began to organize prayer groups in their homes, ignoring the formal structure of the church...The communists of course considered such activities as being 'counter-revolutionary.' Often the local minister, if he discovered his church members holding such meetings, would report them to the local communist authorities. With this kind of situation, church life tended to stagnate completely. The formal church structure is preserved as a shell, but is maintained for the use of meetings or propaganda facility's." [11]

22

III. Infiltration into the Churches of the Free World

We must now consider what is probably the most disgraceful aspect of this whole depressing subject. What are the facts?

"Many American clergymen and church laymen are not aware that the Reds have a well worked-out plan for the infiltration of our churches and church organizations. This infiltration is planned by a secret group of high-level Red agents, labelled the 'Clergical Commission of the Communist Party.' This Red 'commission' is composed of Soviet agents and American Reds, posting as ministers, preachers, and priests, who have fallen away from the church and joined the Communist Party. How do I know about the existence of this Red 'Clergical Commission'? I have reason to know only too well—because in 1945, while posing as a communist for the FBI, I was a member of this Red Commission."

Thus testified Matt Cvetic before the U.S. Congress House Committee in Un-American Activities, July 6-14, 1953.

While this chapter will deal mainly with the American situation, there is no reason to assume that things are very different in Australia. *Communist Penetration Into Australian Churches* is the suggestive title of a pamphlet by the former communist writer V. Borin. And we understand that the Australian League of Rights is about to publish a detailed report on this matter by Mrs. Ann Neill, who posed as a communist agent for Australian counter-intelligence. The former official of the Red Chinese Foreign Office interviewed at length by William G. Goddard, expert on China and formerly with the Department of External Affairs in Canberra, revealed the following:

Teachers, Pastors and Hsi Nao

"Mao has often said that these (teachers and pastors) and not the politicians are the key men in the capitalist world. They do most in shaping the minds of the young. These two, the one in the college, the other in the church, could carry out *hsi nao* (brain-washing) in the capitalist countries. Mao has never been much concerned with adults in China or elsewhere. In China, they can be forced to obey his will or die. In the capitalist countries they will destroy themselves. His one purpose, indeed his supreme objective in China is to create a new humanity, dedicated to communism and completely ignorant of the former values. He looks to selected teachers and pastors to do the same in the capitalist countries."

"But this is impossible this brain-washing, or *hsi nao*, as you call it, will never succeed throughout the free world. I am sure of this."

"I hope you are right. But you would be amazed at the number of teachers and pastors throughout the free world, whose names are already on the list in Peking. And all in regular communication with Peking."

"Are you saying that in the free world there are teachers in the schools and colleges and professors in the universities as well as clergymen in the churches who are agents of communism. I cannot believe it."

"I have seen the mass of teachers and professors in England, America, yes, and in your own country, Australia, who are communist agents. And

I could give you the names of pastors in those same countries who are using their churches for the *hsi nao* I mentioned."[12]

The four-fold Communist Party program of action in the religious sphere was described as follows by the ex-communist, J.Z. Kornfeder, testifying under oath before the House Un-American Activities Committee, on July, 1953.

"(1) The planting of communists among the clergy...

"(2) The channeling of communist clergymen into seminaries where they can train future clergymen who will preach to multiplied thousands;

"(3) The reinterpreting of the Bible is such a way as to support the materialist philosophy of communism...

"(4) The organizing of social action groups of socialist-minded clergymen, who then lead segments of congregations into such political activity as will serve the ultimate purposes of the communist Party."

Union Theological Seminary

The classic example of the damage which even one communist agent can do is that of Harry F. Ward, who for forty years lectured at the influential Union Theological Seminary in New York City. This man, identified by three former communists under oath as having been a member of the Party, influenced countless men who are now clergymen and even prominent theologians and church leaders! This Marxist wrote the official Methodist "Social Creed." The same Marxist ideas were expressed in the social creed prepared for the entire Federal Council of the Churches of Christ in the U.S.A. by a committee of which Ward was a member! And this Marxist propaganda, directed from Moscow, but presented as the position of all the major Protestant churches in the U.S.A., and thus of the tens of millions of Americans whom these churches claim to represent, undoubtedly was an important factor in the perpetration of that Socialist disaster known as the "New Deal".

"It does not require many actual Party members to achieve communist ends. One or two can initiate a measure and then rely on sympathizers, fellow-travelers, and dupes to do the rest!"

Mrs. Helen Sigrist, a former communist, has written:

"The communists I knew felt the greatest contempt for England's Red Dean of Canterbury and other religionists who helped us, even when it was clear that their 'supernaturalism' was little more than words. For all that, we always had a smile and a warm handclasp for the pastor or the Sunday School teacher who wandered our way...Many a church participated in communist-sponsored movements on welfare problems or education or segregation or civil rights."[13]

The ex-communist Manning Johnson testified as follows before the House Un-American Activities Committee (July, 1953):

"It is an axiom in communist organization strategy that if an infiltrated body has 1% Communist Party members and 9% Communist Party sympathizers, with well-rehearsed plans of action, they can effectively control the remaining 90% who act and think on an individual basis. In the large sections of the religious field, due to the idcological

24

poison which has been filtered in by communists and pro-communists through seminaries, the backlog of sympathizers and mental prisoners of socialistic ideology is greater than the 10 percent necessary for effective control."

Ideological Poison
The following samples of "ideological poison" are taken from a 1960 Sunday school quarterly published by one of America's leading Protestant denominations: [14]

"There is no reason why we should not agree with certain Christian values that are also proclaimed by communists such as brotherhood, the abolition of 'the exploitation of man by man', and eventual international peace. Although communists believe that ends justify means, they also believe in some basic Christian values that they hope to achieve after they have conquered the world."

"We have made agreements with many countries which will enable us to establish a ring of missile bases from which nuclear bombs may be shot into any part of Russia. We have armed nations in the North Atlantic Treaty Organizations to increase our strength...Just as Israel needed to place her trust in something greater than the powers of another nation, so must we seek a sounder basis for our national and international security...Primarily our world needs non-military alliances to meet human need...Many church members show no real concern for the conduct of our nation's foreign policy. The policies of massive retaliation and brinkmanship have been called dangerous, but few church leaders have done any thinking that will help us move toward a truly Christian solution of our problem."

"Communism thrives on poverty, and it cannot be defeated by hatred and denunciation. Only unselfish love in the high places of the earth can finally curb it."

"Of course there are many obstacles to peace. For more than a decade the economy of the United States had depended too largely upon the production of armaments...if disarmament upsets business to the extent that earnings are decreased even temporarily, they do not want it." Etc. etc. **ad nauseam.**

Red and Pink Pantheon of "Liberalism"
In other words, the real problem is the un-Christian attitude of the United States! If that were to change, if "unselfish love" were to restrict the production of armaments in the U.S.A., all would be well! There is also propaganda **for** that socialist nightmare, the Welfare State, for the United Nations, whose establishment "lifted millions from despair", and **against** "colonialism" (though nothing is mentioned about the Soviet slave empire), Spain, and Turkey (which are not sufficiently "democratic" but of course there is silence concerning the "democratic" nature of communist states!). The heroes quoted in the quarterly are from the Red and pink pantheon of "Liberalism": Norman Cousins and his wildly Left *Saturday Review*, Albert Einstein, Adlai ("The Appeaser") Stevenson,

Eleanor Roosevelt, the late "Red Queen of America," Mohandas Gandhi, the Hindu, Walter Lippmann, pundit of the Left, Ambassador George F. Kennan, appeasement and compromise monger, etc.

Early in 1960 the House Committee on Un-American Activities held a hearing to deal with the issues raised by the controversial "Air Force Manual." A training manual used by Air Force Intelligence (U.S.A.) had charged that the National Council of Churches was communist-infiltrated. The N.C.C. leadership wired a protest to the chairman of the House Un-American Activities Committee, Rep. Francis E. Walter, for stating that the charges in the manual were quite true. Walter wired back, inviting the N.C.C. leadership to appear before the Committee and discuss the entire matter. The invitation was ignored. The congressional Committee, at its February 25, 1960 hearing, found as follows:

"The chairman issued a statement to the effect that the leadership of the National Council of Churches of Christ in the United States of America had hundreds or at least over 100 affiliations with communist fronts and causes. Since then we have made careful, but yet incomplete checks, and it is a complete understatement. Thus far of the leadership of the National Council of Churches of Christ in American, we have found over 100 persons in leadership capacity with either communist-front records or records of service to communist causes. The aggregate affiliations of the leadership, instead of being in the hundreds as the chairman first indicated, is now, according to our latest count, into the thousands. We have yet to complete our check, which would certainly suggest, on the basis of the authoritative sources of this committee, that the statement that there is infiltration of fellow-travelers in churches and educational institutions is a complete understatement."

Herbert Philbrick, counter-intelligence agent for the (U.S.) Federal Bureau of Investigation, gave this expert testimony concerning the "peace" proposals of the Fifth World Order Study Conference, sponsored by the Department of International Affairs of the National Council of Churches, in 1960:

"I have been a student of communist propaganda for more than 20 years on the basis of that background, knowledge, and study, the 'peace' propaganda now being distributed to local churches in the National Council of Churches, is, in my opinion, the slickest, neatest, trickiest, and the most insidious I have ever seen."[15]

The document "Christian Responsibility on a changing Planet," issued by this Study conference, abounds in pro-communist recommendations. For example:

"With reference to China, Christians should urge reconsideration by our government of its policy in regard to the People's Republic of China. While the rights of the people of Taiwan and of Korea should be safeguarded, steps should be taken towards the inclusion of the People's Republic of China in the United Nations and for its recognition by our government."

On the international ecclesiastical scene a similar situation prevails. We have already seen in a previous section how the "Ecumenical Move-

26

ment," as represented institutionally by the World Council of Churches, the Lutheran World Federation, etc., voluntarily permits itself to be exploited by clerically disguised puppets controlled from Moscow or Peking. The distinguished theological scholar and author, Prof. Arthur Voobus, has, in "An Open Letter to the World Council of Churches and to the Officials of the Lutheran World Federation," dated June, 1963, eloquently protested against this bankrupt and craven mentality which allows the communists to "neutralize" the Christian churches of the West:

Fraternizing With the Attacker

"The decision to admit the so-called Soviet clergymen into the WCC and also the plan to accept them into the membership of the LWF come to me as a shock. Everything that seems to me holy in the Christian faith prompts me to plead with you to reconsider the issue. . .

". . . I myself have been in this inferno and therefore I know what it means for everyone in this situation to think that his fellow Christians in freedom at least take the trouble to know and understand their suffering . . .

"A refusal would also show pity to those few among the so-called Soviet clergymen, who do not play their role voluntarily but under compulsion. This would be a help for them, saving them from the necessity to play a role of hypocrisy and lies. No one has the right to increase their torture after they along with their nations have been abandoned to the Soviets. If, indeed, ecclesiastical organizations cannot live without the Soviets why not act straightforwardly and coopt the officials of the Soviet Secret Police, who now give orders to their underlings in clerical garb?

"It is a tragedy that this fatal decision has been made. It has shaken me to the very depth of my being. As a Christian teacher and scholar I am compelled to take a stand against it. If I could not do that I would see no meaning or sense in my work and life as a Christian. . .

"To create an illusion that there are churches in the Soviet Union that can exist and act as Christian churches and can be represented outside, thereby overlooking the sad realities that are crying to heaven—realities which the Christians should expose—is callousness. But to accept as representatives men who really cannot speak for the sufferers at all but only for their oppressors and persecutors, men who continuously attack the governments of free countries and praise the sincere love of peace of the Soviets, is to ridicule those in agony...

"It cuts deeply into my heart that these sufferers must see the modern priests not only march by on the other side but actually fraternize with the attacker..."

The WCC and Communist Propaganda

The Third Assembly of the World Council of Churches (New Delhi, 1961) voted to approve the report of the section on "Service," which contained the following pro-communist propaganda:

"Years of estrangement and conflict have borne their sad fruit of mutual distrust so that by now nations have false and fixed images of one another...There still remains a suspicion that the other side is out to win completely...Yet responsible leaders in both power blocks do appear to entertain the hope that the two great systems can coexist and even peacefully compete...Another cause of mistrust is the isolation of large parts of mankind from the community of nations...The churches can commend and encourage further human and cultural encounters across political barriers where-by understanding is increased and the common interests of men recognized...Where possible the members of the churches should lead public opinion...in the direction of the objectives of peace and disarmament..." (The New Delhi Report, pp. 105-109).

The crocodile tears about "mutual distrust" imply two patent falsehoods: (1) that the communists do not "trust" the West, and that their "distrust" should be removed by means of further concessions, disarmament etc. This is idiotic. Actually, the Reds are laughing at the infantile policies of the West. They are excellently informed on all developments in the West, and know that they have absolutely nothing to fear. (2) That the West ought to adopt policies based on "trust" in the communists. Anyone who suggests such a thing is either a conscious Red agent or a person in need of some sort of therapy, remedial reading at the very least! One might just as well proclaim it a "Christian duty" to engage, upon request, in a game of roulette with known cheats, gangsters, and cutthroats, at their own tables, and to do so honestly and "trustingly", with one's own and one's children's lives as the stakes! Madness!

Ecclesiastical Busy Bodies

And is Khrushchev, the Ukrainian butcher who has promised to "bury" us, a "responsible leader?" Haven't these ecclesiastical busybodies heard about the communist definition of "co-existence?" and do they not know what every communist knows, namely that "human and cultural encounters" are, for the communists, only a respectable cloak for espionage, sabotage, infiltration, subversion, and propaganda? The "isolation...from the community of nations" undoubtedly refers to the absence of Red China from the U.N.O., "nations" being used here very generously to cover anything from African cannibal tribes to gangster-controlled slave state. Why should Christians help to fulfil Mao Tse Tung's dream of joining the U.N., becoming the leader of the Afro-Asian block, and using that position, among other things, to force Australia to her knees?[16]

The same pro-communist propaganda is expressed even more brazenly and specifically in the "Report of the Committee on the Commission of the Churches on International Affairs (CCIA)", also approved, in substance, by the Assembly. Simply outrageous is the description of "The Christian Peace Conference at Prague" (In Czechoslovakia, under complete communist control!) as a "great work for peace" (p. 267)! What a joke the following solemn suggestion must be in the Kremlin:

"At the earliest possible moment there should be a conference between Christians from various countries with specialists present, especially from the Soviet Union and the United States, who in a completely confidential atmosphere (1) would be able to explain their governments' poli-

28

cies. It is unlikely that ministers or government officials could attend such a conference..." (pp. 266-267).

Imagine the ludicrous scene: Muddle-headed Ecclesiastical do-gooders from the West meet soviet secret police disguised as clergy, and explain "confidentially" the good intentions behind an American or British policy the exact nature of which is understood far better, together with all its ramifications, by the masters of espionage in the Kremlin than by the Western churchmen! And then the Soviet "churchmen" persuade their Western "colleagues" of the good intentions of the Soviet Union!

A Fascinating Debate

The Report also recommends "equitable concessions from both sides" and further appeasement and surrender in Germany (p. 269). A great fuss was made over Angola, while nothing was said of the captive nations behind the Iron Curtain, nor of course was there a word of censure against the "United Nations" for its aggression, brutalities, and suppression of the right of self-determination in Katanga! Such is the "social conscience" of the Ecumenical Movement!

Even a sympathetic student of the entire history of "ecumenical" meddling in politics concludes:

"Yet one may question whether the 'third way' of the World Council really is independent enough, because it seems to have received the readiest approval in the churches of the Western 'neutral' countries. One may also ask whether, for example, the latest development of warfare has affected the policy of the CCIA more than the latest theological studies" (Seppo A. Teinonen, *Missio Politica Oecumenica*, pp. 57-58).

On April 27, 1962, there was held, in Orlando, Florida, U.S.A., a fascinating debate between Bishop Henry I. Louttit (Anglican) and Dr. Carl McIntire (Presbyterian), head of the 72-denomination International Council of Christian Churches. The transcript, obtainable from the 20th Reformation Hour, Collingswood, N.J., U.S.A., is well worth careful study. Dr. McIntire clearly won. He successfully defended the proposition:

"Resolved that the ecumenical movement as represented by the National Council of Churches and the World Council of Churches is giving aid and comfort to the communists."

IV. The Place of the Church in the
Struggle Against Communism

It is not the business of the Church to build or save civilizations. It is true that the work of the Church, which is of a spiritual nature with otherworldly goals, will have effects on human society. But these are in the realm of result, not of purpose. The Church must serve God for God's sake. If this also results, incidentally, in certain beneficial influences on society as a whole, well and good, but these influences are accidental byproducts, not planned goals. The entire realm of civil relations is to be

29

governed by human reason, on the basis of Natural Law and common sense, not on the basis of Revelation. The Church has nothing to say to society as such;—There is no "Christian social order"—she addresses only individuals. Nor has she the slightest interest in prescribing, or regulating the external behavior of non-Christians. She must press the total claim of God in Christ, but in her own sphere, which is not political.

Does this mean that the Church is irrelevant in the struggle against communism? Far from it. In the first place, there are things, which the Church as Church can and must do in this connection, and in the second place, there are things which properly instructed Christian individuals can and must do as patriots and citizens.

Not Meddling in Politics

While the Church has no right to interfere in **purely** temporal, political matters, she does have the duty of warning her members against any moral evil or danger, which may lurk in this or that political issue. Therefore, the Church is not at all "meddling in politics," but is merely doing her divinely assigned duty when she, for example, condemns communism as a moral evil and warns her children against it. Furthermore, if various confused and apostate church leaders or organizations presume to misrepresent Christianity to the public, then it is clearly the right and duty of every congregation and church-body, which regards itself as representing the one, holy, catholic, and apostolic Church of Christ, publicly to counteract such false testimony by word and deed. Spokesmen for the Church have every right, for example, to attack the claims of pacifists and disarmament propagandists as to the Christian nature of their proposals. It is correct Christian doctrine that a lawful state—a communist state can hardly qualify for this title since the very purpose for its existence is inherently immoral, i.e. the abrogation of all principles of Natural Law; Communist "governments" should be viewed as illicit gangster-powers, resting solely on brutality, not on right – has the power of the "sword" (Rom. 13), and may legitimately take human life in the defense of the lives and property of its citizens. It may also wage just wars, namely when the security, liberty, lives, property, etc., of its citizens are threatened. To introduce here texts about "turning the other cheek," which deal with personal reactions, not with the powers of government, is supremely irrelevant and leads to confusion and a silly fanaticism.

Such attitudes are of course quite impossible for church-bodies shot through with rationalism, skepticism, humanism, Darwinism, and Marxist "Social Gospelism". Reinhold Niebuhr, far from conservative himself, hints at the real tragedy when he admits:

"The pathetic clerical Stalinism could not have developed except against the background of a very considerable Marxist dogmatism in the 'liberal' wing of the Protestant churches."[17]

A Disoriented Protestantism

Only a very disoriented "Protestantism" can allow itself to become a tool of the Red Devil. This disorientation was achieved by the same forces that produced Marxism in the first place: Rationalism, materialism, evolutionism. Liberal "theologians", who had thrown overboard the authority of Scripture, along with all Christian dogma, became passionate addicts of a this-worldly "social gospel", decorated with religious slogans but devoid of any firm ethical substance which might have prevented the plunge into collectivist relativism. And it is strange that anyone should have regarded socialism as particularly Christian. After all, from the fact that it is a virtue for me to help my neighbor and share my belongings with him, for the sake of God's love and mercy in Christ, it does not follow that it is virtuous when I am compelled to "share" my goods, or when I ask the government to compel my neighbor to share his goods with me and others! The Seventh Commandment is not cancelled by democratic majorities!

Rev. Alton F. Olsen (Anglican) has written very correctly:

"The real scandal of Christendom is the spiritually bankrupt liberalism, the phony intellectualism, the skeptical neo-orthodoxy, the outright apostasy which is corrupting the very vitals of the professing Church of Jesus Christ...I say that the real scandal of Protestant Christianity today is that men solemnly take ordination vows, dedicating their lives to defending and propagating the historic Christian Faith, only to go out into seminaries and churches and repudiate by their teaching and their preaching these very vows. This is both immoral and dishonest. This is the true scandal of the Protestant Church in our day." [18]

This apostasy must be reversed!

Christian churches must learn anew what it means to be Church, not in order to fight communism, but for its own sake. Churches which truly represent Christ and His one Church, must have clear and certain conceptions of truth and error, right and wrong, and will therefore categorically refuse to inoculate whole populations with that anesthetic of doubt, relativism, and pragmatism, which makes men helpless victims of demagogues and propagandists. It is ironic that it is the modern, uprooted, "critical", "emancipated" mind, not the traditional, Christian, dogmatic one which is utterly uncritical and unrealistic about communism. Strange how sophistication can defeat itself, how reason departs together with faith, and the wisdom of the serpent together with the harmlessness of the dove (St. Mat. 10:-16)!

If Christian laymen would read and study, substitute informed convictions for vague habits and traditions, determine to cut through the fog of confusion to the very core of Truth itself, cost what it may, and then insist on a thorough house-cleaning, on a separation from apostasy, and treason, and enforce these demands with actions, our respectable ecclesiastical hypocrisies would be swept away, and spiritual vigor and dignity would again be associated with the name "Church"!

In the political arena there is much that individual Christian patriots can do. In the Western world governments can generally be made to respond to the wishes of the people. The propagation of correct information must therefore be the prime objective of the anti-communist. People cannot be expected to demand and vote for sensible policies, unless they understand the nature of the communist conspiracy. Speeches, letters to the editor, private conversation, investments in reliable literature, these are effective ways of spreading the truth about communism, and about the best ways of fighting it.

Every anti-communist voter should realize that most elections throughout the British world and the U.S.A. afford the voter an opportunity to choose between two tendencies (often, unfortunately, the choice is only between different degrees of the same tendency): (1) The leftist, socialist tendency, which seeks to centralize government and to put more and more areas of the citizen's lives under the direct or indirect control of an expanding bureaucracy, under the guise of providing necessary or desirable "social services"; (2) An insistence on constitutional, limited, de-centralized government, fiscal responsibility (minimal budget and taxation), and the maximum degree of personal liberty, individual responsibility and initiative (free enterprise) together with a respect for basic rights, including property rights. Christian voters must know that the communists are always on the side of men and parties which represent the first tendency. [19] (I have in my files an official communist pamphlet, distributed prior to the 1963 Queensland election urging voters to support the A.L.P.I.).

Christians must explode the sinister illusion that since "communism is an ideology," it can be fought only with words, not with military and political action. Some criminals can indeed be helped by talking to them. Some can even be converted. But this does not mean that, relying on friendly persuasion, we should abolish all prisons and police forces! Communism is a military and political force, not merely an ideological one, and must be dealt with accordingly. The Christian citizen, unencumbered by ideological fads, "scientific" superstitions, and other mythologies of the times, can and should be the most clear-headed, realistic, and effective anti-communist alive!

(This essay was presented at a seminar on communism conducted by the Australian League of Rights in Toowoomba, Queensland, Australia, October 12, 1963.)

Footnotes:

1 *K. Marx and F. Engels on Religion,* issued by the Central Committee , Communist Party of the Soviet Union, p. 34

2 Quoted in Joseph L. Lichten, "Catholic-Jewish Relations", *Twentieth Century,* Winter, 1963, p. 332.

3 David Easton, "Spirituality and Marx," *The Protestant,* April-May, 1942, p. 55. Cited in the U.S. Congress House Committee in Un-American Activities "Investigation of Communist Activities in the New York City Area—Part 5", p. 223 (U.S. Government Printing Office, Washington: 1953).

4 No footnote

5 Quoted in Major E. Bundy, "The 'Expert' Epidemic", *News and Views,* September, 1962.

6 Carl McIntire, *The Great Debate,* p. 3.

7 William G. Goddard, *The Story of Chang Lao,* p. 34.

8 *Lutheran News* (New Haven, Missouri, U.S.A.), Sept. 23, 1963, p. 7.

9 Ibid.

10 William G. Goddard, op. cit., pp. 60-62.

11 Paul B. Denlinger, "The Christian Church and the Communists in China", *Intelligence Survey,* August, 1963, pp. 4-5.

12 William G. Goddard, op. cit., p. 47.

13 Helen Sigrist, "Communist Program for the Church", *Southern Presbyterian Journal*, March 26, 1958.

14 *Wesley Quarterly*, July, August, September, 1960 (The Methodist Publishing House, Nashville, Tennessee, U.S.A.)

15 "What Do You Know About the National Council of Churches?" (advertisement in *The Greenfield Daily Reporter*, Greenfield, Indiana).

16 William G. Goddard, op. cit. pp. 51 and 63.

17 Quoted in *National Review*, April 9, 1960, p. 2260

18 Alton F. Olsen, "The Real 'Scandal' of Protestantism," *The Episcopal Recorder*, quoted in *Through to Victory*, September, 1963, p. 2.

19 William G. Goddard, op. cit., pp. 46, 64, Cf. Mao Tse Tung, *On People's Democratic Dictatorships*.

Christian News, January 13, 1964

1. What is the communist concept of truth? ____.
2. Karl Marx was born ____.
3. Platonic Paganism insures ____.
4. The Greek word "anti" used figuratively means ____.
5. Liberal religious faith has much in common with ____.
6. To understand the situation behind the Iron Curtain it would be better to ____ than to ____ .
7. The Handbook of the N.C.C.C. does not mention ____.
8. What did Metropolitan Sergius do? ____.
9. The Tikhon Church was strongly ____.
10. In the old Moscow there were more than ____ churches.
11. Yuri Rastvorov testified ____.
12. Who was Metropolitan Nicolai? ____.
13. Metropolitan Nicodim was elected to ____.
14. Who was Janos Peter? ____.
15. Joseph L. Hromradka was identified as ____.
16. The Fourth Assembly of the LWF admitted ____.
17. Latvian Archbishop G Turs was ____.
18. What did J.Z. Kornfeder testify? ____.
19. Where did Harry F. Ward lecture for 40 years? ____.
20. What did ex-Communist Manning Johnson testify? ____.
21. What did the controversial Air Force Manual testify? ____.
22. What did Herbert Philbrick testify? ____.
23. What did Professor Arthur Voobus protest? ____.
24. Dr. Carl McIntire successfully defended ____.
25. Is there a Christian social order? ____.
26. Should the Church condemn Communism as a moral evil? ____.
27. Communist governments should be viewed as ____.
28. What is the real scandal of the Protestant Church today? ____.
29. What are effective ways of spreading the truth about Communism? ____.
30. Christian voters must know that Communists are always on the side of ____.

A CRIMINAL CONSPIRACY

It is a common notion among civilized Western people today, that Communism is another system of government, or of economics, or another social system. And with such notions the idea of legitimacy is always implied. We hear such slogans as these: "One system of government is the same as another. All are imperfect. Therefore one is no more 'right' than another." "Capitalism is not perfect either, so let's not throw stones at Communism."

But Communism is not simply another form of government. It is very much like the *cosa nostra*, the society of gangsters. If this organization were to take control of a nation, it would by no stretch of the imagination be the rightful government of that nation. The people would be compelled to do all in their power to oust the gangsters from power. Communist governments are also criminal societies. Their seizure of power does not make them legal governments. Their power must be destroyed and their lands restored to the people who inhabit them.

Unless we look at Communism in this light, then we need not complain about organized crime.

The statement of the Latvian Evangelical Lutheran Church (*Christian News*, November 4, 1963, p. 3) makes it clear that the criminal and anti-Christian nature of Communism has not changed. The propaganda that says the Reds are assuming a softer line and are easing up on their peoples, is entirely false. Christians and others are more oppressed than ever before. Free Christians cannot stand idly by and approve of oppression of their fellow men and fellow saints. They cannot coddle the oppressors and treat them as legitimate rulers. They will strive with all their might and main against oppression of every sort as long as it exists. And the greater it is the harder will they strive.

The stifled Christians in Red lands need to know that they have not been forgotten. They need to know that our hands are joined with theirs in striking vital blows against total tyranny, "that we, being defended from the fear of our enemies, may pass our time in rest and quietness, through the merits of Jesus Christ, our Savior."

Christian News, November, 4, 1963

1. Comunism is very much like ____.
2. Free Christians cannot stand idly by and ____.
3. The stifled Christians in Red lands need to know____.

PREACHER LIKENS COMMUNISM
TO SATANIC STRATEGY

A Toowoomba clergyman yesterday singled out Communism and certain influential voices in UNESCO's "Mental Health" movement as object lessons in Satanic strategy and craftiness.

Speaking in the Redeemer Lutheran Church, Neil Street, Pastor K. Marquart used modern day developments to illustrate the epistle for the day (Ephesians 8:10-17), on which he was preaching. The sermon dealt with the nature of the Christian's spiritual warfare, and with its weapons.

Pastor Marquart said, in part: "We came into this world with the natural inheritance of sin, death, and damnation, but when God snatched us out of the jaws of hell, in Holy Baptism, we renounced the devil, and declared eternal hostility and war against him. This conflict is total and absolute, and cannot be compromised or arbitrated.

"Recognition of the fact of this conflict is the first condition for victory. At this point we can learn much about Satan's tactics by studying the methods of his personal political representatives, the Communist rulers. For 40 years these men have been engaged in total war against everything that is decent in human civilization. Their one aim, from which they have never wavered, has been and is world conquest, that is, the universal extension of the Red-Hell throughout this globe. They have been at war and have known it.

"In the meantime, however, foolish and cowardly men in the West, who preferred pleasant illusions to hard realities, have kept on telling us that we were not at war, that Communism was willing to co-exist peacefully with Western civilization, that it was possible to bargain with the Reds, that containment and compromise were sufficient safeguards, and other similar delusion. This is precisely how the devil wins wars: he denies that they exist until he has won!

Devil's Trick

"And here is another devil's trick: He knows that our main battleground is our own souls. He has therefore created a climate of opinion which regards all conflict, both external and internal as bad in itself.

"His opinion conditioners are at work to convince us that it is better to tolerate evil than to fight it. Ours is the age of the tranquilizing pill! This creeping moral paralysis is promoted in many ways.

"Popularizes of various half-baked psychological theories, particularly of the Freudian type, bombard the reading public with propaganda to the effect that all emotional conflict is bad. Men and women, imbued with this propaganda, no longer regard it as 'healthy' and 'psychologically sound' to discipline themselves, crucify the flesh with its affections and lusts, in

35

short, to fight Satan in their own souls. Men are taught to surrender to their drives and passions, on the theory that they are merely 'higher' animals anyway.

"You would be shocked to read the hair-raising things written quite openly by representatives of, for example, UNESCO's 'mental health' movement. This school of thought regards all religion as a neurosis (Karl Marx!) from which mankind must be delivered by 'science.'

"The theory is that religion is bad because it sets up moral codes and standards, which create guilt and emotional conflict, and bring about 'priestcraft' – all great evils which must now be rejected as primitive superstitions!"

"And so we actually pay taxes to maintain functionaries of international organizations which seek to destroy and uproot everything that is sacred to us, and to reduce us all to the level of guinea pigs, to be maintained in the name of science, under the Planned Economy and Planned Society of an almighty worldwide slave state! . . .

"Like Communism, the devil wins mainly by means of bluff. When he faces determined resistance, in the name and by the power of God, he backs down. 'Resist the devil, and he will flee from you,' as the Scripture says.

"He has been defeated decisively upon the Cross of Calvary, where 'he who by a tree once overcome (in Eden), likewise by a tree was overcome!' Only arrayed in the divine armaments, listed by the holy Apostle, can we triumph; but by these armaments Christians who are leading defeated, despondent lives can find strength and victory!"

(From the Toowoomba Chronicle and Darling Downs Gazette, November 12, 1962)

Christian News, June 17, 1963

1. What was the one aim of the Communist? ____.
2. How does the devil win wars? ____.
3. Is it better to tolerate evil than to fight it? ____.
4. Is all emotional conflict bad? ____.
5. Where was the devil decisively defeated? ____.

THE MENACE OF PHONY
ANTI-COMMUNISM

The fundamental objection to the September 29, 1969 *Lutheran Witness* article "A Christian Approach to the Menace of Communism" can be compressed into Bernard Baruch's maxim:

"Everyone has the right to his own opinion; but no man has the right to be wrong about the facts!" Our quarrel is not with this or that misinterpretation, but with the underlying, abysmally ignorant and distorted conception of Communism—aptly if insufficiently symbolized by the modish, split-level heading!

We accept without debate the writer's sincerity and the honorableness of the *Witness'* intention. Unfortunately this makes the case not less but more sinister, for Communist propaganda spread by dupes and innocents is far more deadly than the same propaganda spread by known Party organs and members. It is on this principle that the Party practices what Whitaker Chambers called the "conveyor-belt technique": The Party-line, as determined in Moscow, is advocated by a few hardcore secret Communists in key positions, is then picked up by dupes and fellow-travelers and effectively led into the mass communications media. As George Dimitrov put it to the Lenin School of Political Warfare:

"As Soviet power grows, there will be a greater aversion to Communist parties everywhere. So we must practice the techniques of withdrawal. Never appear in the foreground; let our friends do the work. We must always remember that one sympathizer is generally worth more than a dozen militant Communists. . . A writer of reputation, or a retired general, are worth more than 500 poor devils who don't know any better than to get themselves beaten up by the police. Every man has his value, his merit. The writer who, without being a party member, defends the Soviet Union, the union leader who is outside our ranks but defends Soviet international policy, is worth more than a thousand party members" (HUAC, annual report, 1957, p. 2).

But does not the *Witness* piece condemn Communism? Yes, of course. But general condemnations, without an understanding of specific Communist goals and policies, do not worry the Reds in the least. Criminals, after all, fear policemen who detect crime and catch criminals, not policemen who sit in their police stations, fulminating against crime and vice!

Undercover Agent

Recently the writer had the privilege of hearing and meeting Mrs. Ann Neill, who for seven years was a member of the Communist Party, on behalf of the Australian Security Service—whose director, Sir Charles Spry, recently paid a glowing tribute to Mrs. Neill. Mrs. Neill had been ordered by her Communist superiors to keep her Party membership secret , in order to work effectively within various "peace" - organizations. Very interesting was the manner in which she had been ordered to act: If the subject of Communism arose, she would be the first to condemn it, in order to be the more effective in steering the group toward specific pronouncements, actions, and policies, which would advance the current Party line!

The *Witness* article, for all its "unreasoning and hysterical" condemnations of Communism —condemnations not supported by any clear perception and analysis of Communist philosophy, strategy, and tactics—actually propagandizes in favor of the specific Soviet policy of "peaceful co-existence" as effectively as if it had been verbally inspired from Moscow!

I. The Ruse of "Peaceful Co-existence"

Let us deal with the most palpable falsehood first:

"We can be very thankful, for example, that today Moscow has chosen to follow a co-existence policy instead of the implacable repression of Peiping. What if both of these great powers followed the hard line of Red China? How much more difficult for the free world!"

Quite on the contrary! Do citizens rejoice when cutthroats and gangsters don ties and coats and form "legitimate" business fronts or get themselves appointed or elected to public office? Does anyone really believe that open gangsterism is "much more difficult" for the civilized community to handle than the same criminal conspiracy suavely disguising its real nature and purpose behind a benign facade? Is not rather the opposite the case?

It is precisely because the Soviet Union found it "much more difficult" to get its way after incidents like the Hungarian blood-bath of 1956 had alerted and stiffened Western opposition, that the Communists have tried ever since to lull the West into dropping its guard more and more. That is the real meaning of the current "peaceful co-existence" line.

Since there is such a widespread, deliberately cultivated confusion on this subject, let us be quite clear about the elementary facts of the case: The "dispute" between Red China and the Soviet Union is NOT over the question whether violence is or is not permissible. In "One Peaceful Co-existence," published in Moscow in 1961, Khrushchev wrote:

Violence Necessary
"True, we recognize the need for the revolutionary transformation of capitalist society into socialist society. It is this that distinguishes the revolutionary Marxists from the reformists, the opportunists. There is no doubt that in a number of capitalist countries the violent overthrow of the dictatorship of the bourgeoisie and the sharp aggravation of class struggle connected with this are inevitable."

Nor is it at all a question of whether Communism and Western civilization can or ought to live side by side without mutual interference. In

38

1955 Nikita ("Peaceful Co-Existence") Khrushchev said, in Warsaw:

"We must realize that we cannot co-exist eternally, for a long time. One of us must go to his grave. We do not want to go to the grave. They do not want to go to their grave either. So what can be done? We must push them to their grave."

What then is the real issue in the "conflict" over "peaceful co-existence"? Only this: WOULD NUCLEAR WAR AT THIS TIME BE ADVISABLE AS A MEANS OF BRINGING ABOUT THE INEVITABLE WORLDWIDE TRIUMPH OF COMMUNISM? This and only this is really at issue. The conflict is not at all "ideological," but purely tactical. Mao and Khrushchev are both dedicated Marxists, Leninists, Communists. Both believe that they must actively bring about the global victory of Communism. Both believe that any and every means may be used to attain this end. The only question is whether large-scale thermonuclear violence is at this stage a promising tactic, or whether the desired end can be achieved better by other means, such as internal subversion, infiltration, and betrayal (a tactic successfully developed by the Roman general Quintus Fabius Maximus, whence the name "Fabian" Socialism!), and a series of "minor" takeovers, as in Korea, Cuba, Vietnam, Indonesia, Zanzibar, etc. In other words, Peiping and Moscow are quite agreed as to what must happen, i.e. we must be "buried." The only difference is over how this might best be done, i.e. what will be the exact nature of our funeral arrangements, and, possibly, under whose direction.

'Peace' as Surrender

The "Statement of the Soviet Government" which appeared in *Pravda* for August 4, 1963, in answer to Red Chinese denunciations of the Moscow Test Ban Treaty, makes it quite clear that "peaceful co-existence" is merely a tactical measure calculated to bring about the worldwide triumph of the Revolution. The document argues, for instance, that the policy is "both correct and effective." This, in the Marxist-Leninist framework, can only refer to the goal of world-conquest. The treaty is said to be "in the interests of peace and socialism," which of course presupposes the Communist definition of peace as acquiescence to Communist rule. Any act, no matter how violent, is "peaceful," if it advances the interests of the Communist Party, because, as Lenin insisted, Communist morality is determined solely and entirely by the requirements of the revolutionary class-struggle (*Selected Works*, pp. 791 ff.).

Very ominous are those words, from the concluding section of the "Statement": "Science and technology are rapidly developing. And what was unacceptable only yesterday can prove useful, even very useful today."

This echoes Khrushchev's January 6, 1961 speech, which leaves no doubt as to what is meant by "peace".

"The Communist Party of the Soviet Union...will always struggle for universal peace, for the victory of Communism... Communists are revolutionaries, and it would be a bad thing if they did not take advantage of

39

new opportunities that arose and found new methods and forms, providing the best way to achievement of the ends in view."

Stripped of its jargon, the 1963 document is evidently meant to convey to the rulers of Red China as well as to all members of the world-wide conspiracy this simple message:

"Don't worry, we are not compromising. We are in a better positon than you are to judge whether the treaty is to our advantage or not, and we assure you that if it weren't, we wouldn't have signed it. Our policy of 'peaceful co-existence' does not mean that we are in any way betraying the world Revolution. On the contrary, we are merely using it as an effective tactic within the strategy for world-conquest outlined by Lenin. So don't rock the boat. We know what we are doing!"

Lenin—Kind and Gentle?

Very significant is the fact that "peaceful co-existence" is repeatedly called "the Leninist policy," as if to reassure all good comrades that the goal and the basic strategy remain unaltered. This is, in fact, a constant theme with Khrushchev, who said in 1955, in Poland:

"If you think that our smiles mean that we have abandoned the principles of Marx, Engels, and Lenin, you are deceiving yourselves cruelly; we will abandon Communism when the shrimp learns to whistle."

Now, was Lenin, the architect of the "peaceful co-existence" ruse, a humane armchair Communist? He held: "It would not matter a jot if three quarters of the human race perished; the important thing is that the remaining quarter should be Communists."

And when Maxim Litvinoff, who secured U.S. recognition of the Soviet Union, in return for worthless paper assurances, said: "You know our principles; promises that we make to capitalist countries are not binding," he was merely following Lenin, who wrote:

"The so-called cultural elements of Western Europe and America, are incapable of comprehending the present state of affairs and the actual balance of forces; these elements must be regarded as deaf-mutes and treated accordingly...

"We must, (1) in order to placate the deaf-mutes, proclaim the fictional separation of our government ...from the Cominterm... (b) Express a desire for the immediate resumption of diplomatic relations with capital countries on the basis of complete non-interference in their internal affairs...

"Again, the deaf-mutes will believe it. They will even be delighted and fling wide-open their doors, through which the emissaries of the Cominterm and Party Intelligence agencies will quickly infiltrate into these countries disguised as our diplomatic, cultural, and trade representatives...

"Capitalists the world over and their governments will in their desire to win the Soviet market, shut their eyes to the above-mentioned activities and thus be turned into blind deaf-mutes. They will furnish credits, which will serve as a means of supporting the Communist parties in their countries, and, by supplying us with materials and techniques which are not available to us, will rebuild our war industry, which is essential for our future attacks on our suppliers. In other words, they will be laboring to prepare their own suicide..." (Quoted in M. Dies, Martin Dies' Story, p. 26).

The Witness is deluding itself, and worse, its readers, by pretending that there is anything to be "thankful" for in Moscow's current method of victory by stealth.

II. Does Communism Change?

"Communism as a political-economic system has developed differently in countries in which it has gained control—communism is not a change-less monolithic structure. It has changed, it can change, it will change." Thus saith the *Witness*. No more ignorant nonsense could have been written.

In the first place, strictly speaking, "Communism as a political-economic system" does not exist anywhere on earth, as the Communists are the first to insist. All that exists is a collection of countries in which varying degrees of Socialism are maintained by means of military terror. (Unlike Western egg-heads, the Communists realize that Socialism simply does not work—they have tried it—and they are therefore forced, particularly in times of crisis, to make concessions to the profit motive, in order to rescue production from utter collapse!) According to Communist theory, this intermediate period of Socialism, enforced by the "dictatorship of the proletariat," i.e. of the Communist Party, must of necessity continue until (1) the whole world shall have been brought under the complete control of the Party; and (2) the latter shall have succeeded, by means of mass-extermination and brain-washing ("education") in producing a new humanity, "which will voluntarily give according to ability and receive according to need, thus enabling the admittedly harsh dictatorship, indeed, the entire machinery of government, to wither away," as the theory puts it, with quaint piety!

Change and Decay

Now, the fact that different times and circumstances require different methods of warfare, and that the various countries swallowed by the Communist monster are found in different stages of digestion, does not at all mean that "Communism changes." Anyone who knows anything about Communism knows that what changes are only particular methods, and details of tactics, never the goal itself, or even the grand strategy of world conquest, as laid down by Lenin. Changed appearances under changed conditions is the most obvious truism in the world for the point of view of **Dialectical Materialism**, which is the technical term for the philosophy of Communism. Now, people who do not understand **dialectics**, the very cornerstone of the rigid Marxist creed, have no business trying to be helpful to other blind men in this regard—especially in the vicinity of ditches.

Anyone who really wonders why Communism apparently "changes,"

41

should read Lenin's diatribe on the "Left radicalism" for instance, which states the famous zigzag doctrine of advance by means of apparent retreats. Also note this tidbit: "Inexperienced revolutionaries often think that lawful methods of warfare are opportunistic... but that (only) illegal methods are revolutionary. But this is incorrect. Revolutionaries who do not know how to combine illegal methods of warfare with **all** lawful ones, are very bad revolutionaries." Khrushchev is neither a bad nor an inexperienced revolutionary!

Simply flabbergasting is the casual, matter-of-fact way in which specific Communist policy objectives are slipped to the reader of the *Witness* piece:

"People become tremendously exercised over diplomatic recognition of Red China, trade with Communist Cuba, or selling wheat to Communist Russia. Many arguments can be offered both for and against decisions on these highly controversial issues."

After asking how "we as Christians" should "approach such questions," the article develops the distinction between Church and State in such a manner as to suggest, obviously, the following line of thought: Since the State has functions and methods differing from those of the Church, one would not expect in the actions of the former a purity of principle which is really appropriate only for the latter. The State must act "realistically," and therefore should be expected to answer such questions as the above (recognition of Red China, etc.) in a manner which may not please Christians from an ideological standpoint. In other words, we should not be disturbed by, but expect and "understand" governmental compromises and appeasement on these issues! That is clearly the whole trend of the argument, though the actual formulations are impeccably cautious. The suggestion that Communists should be treated as individual "people," – logically a dreadfully irrelevant banality, since it is governmental action that is being considered,–merely reinforces the sentimental blur with which religionists are nowadays expected perpetually to prevent having the Communist issue brought into clear focus.

Realism, not Idealism, the Issue

And of course it is utter nonsense to suggest, as the article does, that the Conservative positions regarding recognition of Red China, trade with Red Cuba, etc., rest essentially on religious and moral idealism— with the implication that they therefore merit no more attention in the formulation of national policy than, say, Seventh Day Adventist aversion to coffee! Actually, the Conservative position rests upon a realistic grasp of Communist philosophy and strategy. The real objection to the recognition of Red China, etc. is not that such facts are bad theology, but that they are bad politics. They are stupid and suicidal precisely because they misunderstand the nature of the Red barbarity and its assault upon civilization. Recognition of Red regimes merely bestows a coveted prestige, which is then exploited very effectively in the propaganda war. Also, political legitimacy with all its works and all its pomp offers ideal opportunities for the diplomatic immunization of the subversive apparatus' nerve

42

centers in the Western world. As for trade, any informed person knows that this is regarded merely as an aspect of political—economic warfare by the Reds. It is precisely the State as State, then, which must firmly reject, on purely tactical, political grounds, any suggestion of compromise in such matters.

The New Idolatry

Given clear thinking, however, the State-Church distinction favors not Liberalism, as the *Witness* imagines, but Conservatism. Has not America been retreating before Communism for lo, these many years, precisely because it insisted on acting not as a State, but as a kind of secularist, Rooseveltian Church, with Socialism as its official mythology and the Schlesingers, Lippmanns, etc. as its prophets? The reason for America's failure to win the cold war is not too much political realism, but too much of the wrong, pink-eyed, mutton-headed ideology—plus a dash of reason to be sure!

Strange to say, while the state has been growing into an intolerant secular Church, bitterly persecuting all who deviate from its narrow Liberal (i.e. totalitarian)creed, the churches have been behaving more and more like Machiavellian states, tolerating any and every "point of view" for the sake of organizational and budgetary stability and solidarity! What a mad, topsy-turvy state of affairs! If only the State would go back to being State, and the Church to being Church! The forthcoming American election for the first time in thirty years offers the American people a magnificent opportunity to take a big step in the right direction.

Christian News, November 2, 1964

1. Every man has the right to his opinions but no man has the right to be ____.
2. Communists spread propaganda by ____.
3. The *Lutheran Witness* actually propagandized in favor of ____.
4. "Peaceful co-existence" was a tactic to ____.
5. What kind of ignorant nonsense did the *Lutheran Witness* promote? ____.
6. The Communists recognized that ____ does not work?
7. ____ is the technical term for Communism?
8. Recognition of Red Regimes merely ____.
9. Churches have been developing more and more into a Machiavellian state by ____.

RELIGIOUS SOCIALISM

"Christian Social Action", a *Lutheran Witness* editorial of Dec. 8, 1964, might just as well have appeared in *The Christian Century*. It certainly does not say anything that is particularly Scriptural. On the contrary, the Social Gospel outlook seems to be taken for granted by such expressions as "the degree of involvement the church ought to seek in social issues". In other words, it is only a question of degree. "The church's" right to be involved in "social issues" at all is not even questioned.

What is entirely overlooked is Luther's Biblical distinction between God's "Kingdom on the Right," the Church, and His "Kingdom on the Left," the socio-political order. It is a Roman and Calvinistic delusion that the Church must guide, influence, and, if possible, direct the functioning of society. No such program will be found in the New Testament! The Church has its tasks and methods. The former administers supernatural treasures, the Gospel and the Sacraments, for men's salvation, while the latter takes care of temporal order and justice, on the basis of Natural Law, reason, and experience—not revelation! The things of God and the things of Caesar should not be mixed

It is true that Christians, as subjects or citizens, owe their governments and countries loyal service and support (see the Table of Duties in the Catechism). This means that Christians will, in their capacity as citizens, advocate, support, and promote such policies and measures as are most conductive to public order and justice (Augsburg Confession XVI). The Church as Church, however, has nothing to say to the State as such, nor has it any divinely-given blue-print for society.

Intellectual Snobs

When the *Witness* appeals to Martin Luther King, the National Lutheran Council, the L.C.A's "Board of Social Ministries," and the World Council of Churches, it becomes very clear that it is not just a general Calvinistic Church-State mixture, but the specific, rather unsavory Religious Socialism, known as the Social Gospel, which is being worked into the Missouri Synod.

Dr. Martin Luther King has himself recorded his indebtedness to Walter Rauschenbusch (*The Christian Century*, April 13, 1960, p.440). Now, who was Rauschenbusch? He was the real founder of the Social Gospel in America. His "theology" was simply a religiously sugarcoated socialism. Stormer's *None Dare Call It Treason*—for intellectual snobs of course facts contained in books they dislike simply don't exist; Orwell's Memory Hole, you know! — traces the connection between Rauschenbusch and Fabian Socialism. And Harry Ward, later identified as a communist, wrote the Methodist "Social Creed," the Marxist principles of which were repeated in the official social creed of the whole Federal Council of

Churches by a committee of which Ward was a member! Transmission of Socialistic Propaganda through the religious leadership of the country undoubtedly helped the "New Deal" considerably. And Lutheran News has already reported the fact that the Religious Establishment was against Goldwater in 1964 and undoubtedly played a major part in his defeat.

Contributing to Communist World Conquest

The ecclesiastic "Social Action" which the *Witness* is now recommending to its readers, has in the past been entirely misdirected and has unwittingly made a tremendous contribution to Communist world-conquest. The bitter irony is that many sincere people have been imagining that they were merely putting the Christian Faith into action socially and economically, when in actual fact Christianity was merely the verbal decoration on the Socialist ideology, which at the bottom is atheistic, materialistic, and anti-Christian! The Christian Faith hasn't been applied to society at all; Socialist ideology has been applied to Christianity, instead! And modern theology itself—having jettisoned the historic Christian content in an effort to be "relevant'—is more irrelevant than ever! (See "The Irrelevance of Theology," *The Christian Century*, Dec. 30, 1959).

And now comes something which should shock all sincere members of the Religious Establishment into sudden awareness of the horrible reality: Richard H. Rovere, the prominent political analyst, and himself certainly no Goldwater Tory, has published a book *The American Establishment* (London: Rupert Hart-Davis), the following statements of which are among the most significant written this century:

"The Establishment is a general term for those people in finance, business, and professions, largely from the Northeast, who hold the principal measure of power and influence in this country irrespective of what administration occupies the White House... (It is) a working alliance of the near-socialist professor and the internationalist Eastern banker calling for a bland bi-partisan to national politics....

"Summing up the situation at the present moment, it can, I think, be said that the Establishment maintains effective control over the Executive and Judicial branches of government; that it dominates American education and intellectual life; that it has very nearly unchallenged power in deciding what is and what is not respectable opinion in this country. Its authority is enormous in organized religion (Roman Catholics and fundamentalists Protestants to one side), in science, and indeed, in all learned professions except medicine." (My emphasis)

Clowns in a Farce

There we have it. Hundreds of well-meaning Eccleslsatics are eagerly promoting the social (ist) programme of the National Council of Churches, in the belief that they are making Christianity "relevant," and that, like the prophets of old, they are announcing God's judgment upon

45

society etc. How galling to realize that far from being prophets coura-geously denouncing the iniquities of their times, these people are merely instruments sub-serving the purposes of the "working alliance of the near socialist professor and the internationalist Eastern banker" (isn't that exactly what the late Major C. H. Douglas, the founder of Social Credit, had been claiming for years, in his brilliant books?) who decide "what is and what is not a respectable opinion in this country," and whose "au-thority is enormous"—where? Among the "irrelevant," socially "irrespon-sible" Fundamentalists? No! In that very same "organized religion" which is supposed to be so prophetic and "socially responsible"! Perhaps Ro-vere's book will help sincere men here and there to realize that whereas they fancied themselves solemn heroes in a tragedy, they have not been given the whole script, which, in the larger perspective makes them but clowns in a farce!

Good Samaritans

There are of course socio-political issues with moral aspects, on which it is the Church's duty to speak—not for the State's benefit, as "Con-science of the nation," but for the guidance of Christians. When, for ex-ample, an apostate, this—worldly ecclesiasticism advances, in the name of Christianity, some Socialist economic scheme, or some pro-Communist policy (disarmament, "peaceful co-existence," etc.) it is the duty of the faithful Church to tear the Christian mask off this hoax. And it is cer-tainly the duty of the Church to warn her members against ideologies (Fabian and Marxist Socialism) which, no matter how "respectable" among the opinion molders of "the near-socialist professor and the inter-nationalist Eastern Banker," are irreconcilably opposed to the Christian world view.

When it comes to specific issues – like the fashionable obsession with "race relations?" The Church too must demand of her members (not of the State) justice and charity. But this does not mean agitation for dis-astrously totalitarian "Civil Rights" legislation, as Dr. Hamann has pointed out in his penetrating article "Racism" (AUSTRALIAN THEO-LOGICAL REVIEW, September, 1963).

And the *Witness* is quite right in saying: "More than sporadic charity is needed." But the solution proposed, that "The church" as such "must risk involvement in all areas of life that matter to people" is Calvinistic and unacceptable. Hospitals, relief-centers, welfare—clinics, etc., ought to be undertaken by societies within the Church. And it is important that our preaching be such as to inspire Christians to genuine compassion for all humanity—and not just abstractly, but concretely. Genuine Christian compassion, free of cant and pose, will never be "respectable," but must—like St. Francis – expect active opposition from the Establishment in Church and State. But, like St. Francis, it will find ways and means of being Good Samaritans to suffering humanity in the Name of the Son of Man!

Christian News, January 11, 1965

1. Must the Church guide the functions of society? ____.
2. The *Lutheran Witness* is the official publication of ____.
3. The things of God and the things of Caesar should not be ____ .
4. Does the Church have a divinely given blueprint for society? ____.
5. King recorded his indebtedness to ____.
6. For intellectual snobs facts contained in books they dislike simply ____.
7. Harry Ward, later identified as a Communist, wrote ____.
8. Socialist ideology at the bottom is ____.
9. What is more irrelevant than ever? ____.
10. Hundreds of Ecclesiastics are ____.
11. What had Major C. H. Douglass been claiming? ____.
12. Genuine Christian compassion like St. Francis must ____.

THE SAME BAD SEED

Marxism and Modern Theology Sprout from a Single Source
Reverend Kurt Marquart
The Manion Forum

Member of Commission on Theology and Inter-Church Relations, Lutheran Church of Australia

DEAN MANION: Must Communism conquer the churches? Where is the battle line today? The answers are linked to the fate of human freedom here and all over the world. With me at the microphone now is a learned and eloquent theologian. During the past three weeks he has been discussing these questions with courage and conviction before large audiences in all parts of the country.

The Reverend Kurt Marquart is a Lutheran minister, who is pastor of Good Sheperd Lutheran Church in Toowoomba, Queensland, Australia. He received his theological education at the St. Louis Seminary of the Lutheran Church, Missouri Synod, and has been lecturing in the United States under the co-sponsorship of the Lutheran fellowship known as The State of the Church (Missouri Synod) and the Evangelical Lutheran Synod.

Shortly after he was born, Reverend Marquart's family fled from the Communist invasion of his native Estonia and took refuge in Austria. In 1945 the Communists forced them to move again. In 1949 the family arrived in the United States.

Reverend Marquart we are delighted to have you here on the Manion Forum.

REVEREND MARQUART: Thank you. Dean Manion, for having me on your program.

DEAN MANION: Reverend Marquart, currently the Christian- Communist dialogue, so called, is very much in the news. How do you react to this effort for "understanding"?

REVEREND MARQUART: I react particularly, and especially in two ways. In the first place, I react to it in the same way as I would react to the proposition of dialogue with Nazis and Fascists. It seems to me that Fascism and Nazism killed six million Jews[1]—Communism killed about one hundred million people. Dialogue with one set of mass murderers, it seems to me, is on the same plane as dialogue with another set. Whether it is national socialism or international socialism, it's the same thing, ultimately.

But, my second reaction would be that I realize from a study of Marxism that anything that the Communists do they do for a purpose. They regard conversations and dialogues as weapons in the cause of their ultimate world conquest. I don't propose to help them achieve this.

48

Now, what do they have to gain? They have to gain prestige among, shall we say, the uncommitted and the confused in the West. This prestige they hope to gain by being treated as equals and respectable partners in respectable dialogue. A second purpose they intend to achieve is to demoralize and further suppress those whom they already enslave because when these people see their captors and slave-masters being treated as respectable partners in dialogue in the West then they will despair of all hope of even being understood.

To my mind this is adding insult to injury–passing by instead of being the Good Samaritan, passing by without seeing and without wanting to see on the other side. And, may I add that I believe that a prominent Jesuit Priest in Germany, Father Rahmer, who had been participating in these dialogues, has refused to attend the last one because he realized that it was being exploited for Communist ends.

DEAN MANION: Pastor Marquart, you know of course that Christians have a commission to go "into all the world." This would seem to oblige Christians to speak with all and to witness to all. How then do you reconcile the position you have just outlined—a refusal to dialogue with Communists—and the Christian commission to go into all the world?

REVEREND MARQUART: Yes, that's a very good question. But remember, there are two sides to this. The same Lord who said "go into all the world" also said "Don't cast pearls before swine."

I cannot accept as equal partners in dialogue people to whom I must bear witness and to whom I must proclaim the Christian Gospel. I am perfectly prepared to have dialogue in this sense, that I am prepared to defend the truth of the Christian faith against the religion of Communism. But the trouble is, this kind of dialogue the Communists don't want. They want to talk with people who are not going to point out their fallacies, but who will merely provide them with an easy and cheap propaganda weapon, a platform, a sounding board for Communist propaganda.

In Australia, we have had a number of cases to show that the Communists are not interested in a genuine facing of Christianity and Communism. For instance, the Christian Anti-Communist Crusade—a New South Wales branch—last year received a challenge from the Communist Party there to debate any aspect of Communism that they chose. The Crusade sent a letter back stating that they would be very happy to discuss the proposition—to debate the proposition—"The Record of Communism is indefensible." Well, it died a natural death and the Communists refused to discuss this proposition.

So, when people arise who wish really to press the truth of the Christian faith against Communism, the Communists lose all interest in dialogue. They wish only to talk with people who will allow them to exploit them for propaganda purposes.

Marxism And Modern Theology
Have Common Root
DEAN MANION: Reverend, today churches of all denominations are

experiencing much unrest in many different ways—unrest because of apparent changes from the traditional, unrest because of the trend in the Ecumenical Movement, etc. Would you care to comment on the condition of Christendom at the present time?

REVEREND MARQUART: I feel that much of the unrest is due to the tragedy that has befallen Christendom in the last 200 years, namely, the tragedy that began with rationalism—the idea that human reason is supreme. When this idea came into the churches, people began to think that mankind had now become of age, no longer needed what they called superstitions, doctrines received on authority, but now could work things out on the basis of human reason alone.

That meant, of course, that there was no more need for a Divine Revelation, for authority and truth. The more this vicious system worked itself into the European churches through the universities where the clergy were trained, the more there came about a general collapse in all revealed truth, in all definite truth, and today people—most people—no longer believe that there is such a thing as revealed truth, only insights, aspects, interpretations and emphases, that there is no God-given truth. And, of course, if there are no standards, then there has got to be confusion. This follows naturally.

It seems also that the political and the religious trends are closely connected because Marxism arises out of Hegel and modern theology arises out of Hegel too. I read a very interesting essay recently by John Montgomery. He covers very nicely this fact that all of modern theology is based upon a philosophical system. For instance, German idealism of the last century: a philosophical system which is already today antiquated. The whole modern theology is based upon this, and, as I say, the religious and the secular confusion seems to arise out of the same sources—German philosophical backgrounds which today are antiquated.

DEAN MANION: From what you have said, I would conclude that what we know as the current forward thrust in theology is in reality a backward movement. Is that right?

REVEREND MARQUART: Yes, that's always the fate of a theology which is bound to human opinion, because sooner or later it becomes unfashionable. I am reminded of what Chesterton said, he said many profound things and he said them wittily. He said, "We don't need a creed which is right when we are right, but we need a creed which is right when we are wrong."

DEAN MANION: You mentioned that there is a common background in both Communism and in modern theology—that both owe something to Hegel—do you then see a Communist influence in the modern church?

REVEREND MARQUART: Well yes, in what is thought to be the church, there seems to be some Communist influence. It is reasonable to assume that if the Communists are working to infiltrate the church, they are having some degree of success. I am thinking of the testimony of a former Communist by the name of Kornfeder, who testified before an American Congressional Committee that he used to be apart of a so-called Clergical Commission of the Communist Party in the United

50

States, whose object it was to infiltrate the churches to boost the ends of the Communist Party from within the church. He mentioned a fourfold program and two of the points, I remember, were pushing the Communist social program through the churches, and to further ways of interpreting the Bible which would favor the Marxist interpretation of things.

DEAN MANION: Reverend Marquart, many clergymen, and many laymen, too, are contending that the war in Viet Nam is an immoral war. How do you look upon the current conflict in Viet Nam?

Objecting Clergymen Lack Christian Charity

REVEREND MARQUART: I believe it is very immoral—on the part of the Communists. But, I think that what the Americans and the Australians are doing in Viet Nam is comparable to the Good Samaritan if he would have rescued the victim from the murderers who were beating him up.

But now, for some clergymen to be standing aside as they see the poor Vietnamese being terrorized and being brutally assaulted by the Viet Cong, and nothing is said. Then along come the American Marines and they liberate, or try to liberate the victims, and now these clergymen wave their umbrellas and say "naughty boys you mustn't use violence." It seems to me that this is contrary to all Christian justice and charity.

The church has always taught on the basis of the New Testament that there is such a thing as a just war, and it seems to me that few wars in history have been more just than wars against such an obviously oppressive and unjust tyranny which denies all natural law as that of the Communists.

You have Romans 13, which makes it quite clear that he—that is the government, the power—bearith not the sword in vain. In other words, the sword is not to be used just to knight somebody or for ceremonial processions, the sword is to be used to keep order, to protect the citizens in their property and in their life and safety.

This is what they are doing in Viet Nam. They are defending a legitimate society against hostile foreign invaders and oppressors, and this is perfectly just on Christian principles.

DEAN MANION: In Australia you live much closer to Viet Nam than we do in this country. How do the Australian people feel about the Viet Nam War?

REVEREND MARQUART: It is difficult to generalize on the basis of one's own observations, but I would simply refer you to the outcome of the last election which was Mr. Holt's first election as Prime Minister—after Sir Robert Menzies. This election was significant because the leader of the opposition—the Labor Party, made it his business to make it quite clear that the real issue of the election was the Viet Nam war.

He promised, if elected, to pull our boys out of Viet Nam. He went up and down the country campaigning against Viet Nam, and said he would bring the government down on this very issue. The result of the election was that the Labor Party was massively defeated at the polls, lost even *more* heavily than the government had dared to hope. This, I think, is the answer of the Australian people to the question.

DEAN MANION: Reverend, many people in this country contend that we should withdraw our military forces from Viet Nam. In your opinion, what would be the result on Southeast Asia of the withdrawal of American and Australian troops from Viet Nam?

REVEREND MARQUART: This is outside my theological competence, but as a human being I would say it would be a disaster because, particularly in the Far East where prestige and face matters a great deal, it would be taken as a tremendous victory for Communism; it would inevitably mean that the governments of Southeast Asia will have to lean more toward China —I mean Red China, of course.

DEAN MANION: Ecumenism and ecumenicity are in the news today. What is your reaction to the current clamor for ecumenicity?

REVEREND MARQUART: That is a very complex issue. I am, of course, in favor of true unity, and as a servant of Christ and of His church, I would be delighted to do anything in my power to advance true unity and understanding among Christians. At the same time, I fear, in fact, I know, that much of what passes for ecumenicity is really something based on compromise rather than truth. It is not an inner unity that is being created but an outward union, which is a poor substitute, in fact, a deceptive substitute.

I do not believe that this is what the Lord wanted nor what can be documented from the New Testament. Truth there is primary, and the Lord never said that where there are two or three million gathered in my name there will I be in the midst of them. We have to go by truth not by numbers.

To conclude, I would say that I see a great danger that many today, in what is called the Ecumenical Movement, confuse the humility of Jesus Christ with the skepticism of Pontius Pilate, who said, "What is truth?" Much church politics seems to be based on the proposition that nobody can really know what the truth is, that it isn't there, for all practical purposes, and therefore we might as well get together on the basis, not of unity, not of conviction, but on the basis of compromise, of skepticism.

DEAN MANION: Thank you. Reverend Kurt Marquart, of Queensland, Australia, for this most informative interview. My friends, in my 13 years at this microphone, I have never heard a more precise and learned analysis of the conflict now raging between Communism and organized religion, namely, the churches of all denominations. For all those who wishfully believe that this killing conflict can peacefully be composed, this broadcast is required reading. Every minister of religion, including your own, must have this broadcast. Sound tapes and written scripts are available at the Manion Forum.

Christian News, December 11, 1967

[1] Kurt Marquart, along with such confessional Lutheran theologians as Paul Burgdorf, Henry Koch, Rudy Kurz, Paul Neipp, Walter Maier, Wallace Schulz, and others who opposed Hitler and the horrors of Nazism but who also examined the evidence maintained that there was no evidence to prove that the Germans during WWII exterminated some 6

million Jews, most of them in gas chambers. See "Marquart and the Six Million Holocaust," "Auschwitz-The Final Count," "Auschwitz Eye Witness Says Germans Did Not Gas Six Million Jews," *Christian News*, March 21, 2011 and "Christians – Tell the Truth" *Christian News Encyclopedia*, Vol. V pp. 3617-3639; and "Christians Defend the Truth – Reject all Hoaxes," *Christian News Encyclopedia*, Vol V, pp. 3974-3991.

Many Lutheran theologians, however, agree with LCMS President Matthew Harrison, who insisted in the LCMS's January, 2013 *Lutheran Witness* that it is a fact that the Germans exterminated six million Jews during WWII. KFUO's *Issues, Etc.* announced that the Germans during WWII exterminated "Six million Jews" *Issues Etc.* said were living in Germany during WWII. Population figures show that there were less than 300,000 Jews living in Germany during WWII.

1. Communism killed about ____.
2. Communists are not interested in a genuine facing of ____.
3. Communism and modern theology have a ____.
4. The unrest befallen Christendom in the last 200 years began with ____.
5. Today most people no longer believe that there is any revealed ____.
6. John Montgomery showed that all modern theology is based on ____.
7. The current thrust in theology is in reality ____.
8. We don't need a creed which is right when we are right but a creed which is right when we ____.
9. The Church has always taught that there is such a thing as ____.
10. Much of what passes today for ecumenicity is ____.
11. What did Dean Manion say about Kurt Marquart? ____.

"THE FATE OF CHRISTIANS UNDER COMMUNISM"

Editor's Note: This address was given at the Second Annual Seminar of The Australian League of Rights held in Brisbane, Australia, May 11, 1968.

It is reproduced from "Christianity and Communism," a 45 page booklet available from the Australian League of Rights, Queensland Council, P. O. Box 3, Paddington, Queensland, 4064. $1.00.

Pastor Marquart was born in Estonia but left that unhappy country after the Communist take-over had begun. He received his theological education in the U.S.A. His mother and step-father had been born in Russia. With this back-ground and further research, he presented his paper.

His paper examines how communist theory about religion has worked in practice. The paper clearly answers the question: "Is there freedom of religion in communist countries?" After discussing this question, the paper then analyses and documents how the communists have been able to inject their propaganda into the World Council of Churches.

I. Persecution: A Study in Depth

It is difficult for those who have not directly experienced Communism to comprehend the horror of it all. Allied soldiers, who as a result of the infamous Yalta Agreement, had to force Soviet citizens "liberated" from German captivity at the end of World War II, to return to the Workers' Paradise, reacted with utter bewilderment and incomprehension when most of these people not only refused to go back "home", but resorted to the most desperate measures to avoid this fate. I myself shall never forget the pathetic spectacle I witnessed in 1945, of a two-mile stream of Russians, simple workers and peasants in the main, fleeing into the woods with what few belongings they could carry, to avoid being sent back to the Soviet Union. One of our friends, a Russian engineer, went back to the camp to help rescue some others, and was caught by the British soldiers whose distasteful duty it was to enforce these inhuman mass-deportations. When the man vehemently resisted "repatriation", the British officer in charge asked him if he realized that he could be sent to goal for five years if he refused to co-operate.

Our friend explained that he would gladly go to prison rather than return to the Red hell! He served five years.

In other camps, also in the American occupation zone, even more terrible scenes took place. When the men had been herded like cattle onto trucks, the women would lie down on the road in front of the trucks, and had to be removed at bayonet point. Not infrequently mothers would kill their children, and then slash their own wrists, if there was no other way out Such unparalleled mass desperation testifies unanswerably to the utter contempt for human life practiced in the name of the brotherhood of man by the most brutal, most cynical, most inhuman regime of modern times, if not of all history. This sober truth must be hammered again and again into the consciences of those manipulated innocents who yap incessantly about South Africa, Rhodesia - and of course Vietnam!

Statistics and "objective" reports of surface events can never do justice to the quality, the dreadful depth dimension, of the Communist persecution of the Church. It is only the *intensive* aspect, the concrete detail, the individual agony, that can fill the impersonal, *extensive* accounts with terrible meaning. This then shall be the theme of the first Section of this paper.

The first item I should like to introduce in evidence is an eye-witness account, by R. Nilostonski, of the barbarities perpetrated in its early years by the Red Counter-Revolution (Ulyanov ["Lenin"], Bronstein ("Trotsky"), Rosenfeld ["Kamenev"], & Co. replaced not the Czar but the first democratic, republican government of Russia!) in the South of Russia.

The book reproduces actual photographs of mutilated corpses, and indicates, on a map of Kiev, the precise locations of the various human *abattoirs* operated by the Communist butchers. In those early years the Red plenipotentiaries in those regions were simply criminals and sadists of the worst sort, who murdered for pleasure. There were nightly orgies in the human slaughterhouses. These were run by the "Che-Ka"(for "Chresvychainaya Comnissiya"or "Extraordinary Commission", in charge of liquidating "counter-revolutionaries"). The "che-kists", many of them drug-addicts and degenerates of all sorts, would gather every evening with their cronies, mainly prostitutes of both sexes, and would spend the night drinking, and torturing their unhappy victims. When the monsters became bored, or tired, or too drunk, their human prey was finally dispatched. Usually the unfortunates were driven naked into the cellar, and there forced to lie down in the revolting mass of blood and brains that covered the floor, to receive some bullets or have their skulls crushed.

Christian clergy were generally tormented with a barbed-wire "crown of thorns", and were often stoned or crucified. Meanwhile the murderous gang would laugh and do their utmost to mock the sufferers and increase their pain in various ways. Fortunate indeed were those who were simply gunned down in their churches! The "Che-Ka's" of the various cities developed their own specialties of bestiality, and vied with one another in the invention of ever more devilish devices. In Voronesh, for instance, people were forced, naked, into barrels, into which nails were then driven, and the barrels rolled about. Charkov favored the "removing of gloves", i.e. scalping of the hands. In Poltava the degenerate sailor, "Grishka Prostitutka" on one day alone impaled 18 monks. The victims were made to sit on sharpened stakes which gradually pierced the body in the most painful possible manner. This method enjoyed wide popularity.

Elsewhere a pipe would be placed against the victim's body, a rat inserted into the pipe, and then the frenzied beast would be driven with fire to gnaw its way into the human body. At least in one place (Kiev) a row of victims would have their heads crushed, and the next row was

55

forced to kneel behind them and to eat the brains out of their skulls!

I have reached, perhaps even exceeded, the limits of what is mentionable. Much more happened. No wonder the units of the White Volunteer Army under Generals Wrangel and Denikin, when surrounded by the Reds, would never surrender, but would first of all shoot their nursing sisters (for whom the Reds reserved their most inhuman outrages), their wounded, and any members of their families accompanying them! When the White Volunteers temporarily liberated Kiev, a full judicial inquiry was undertaken into the mass murders of the "Che-Ka". No fewer than 12,000 people had been slaughtered. Some inhabitants insisted that the number was between 30,000 and 40,000. The stench was impossible, and gas-masks had to be used near the places of horror. Hardened British sailors (of the warships "Montrose" and "Steadfast" for instance) said that they could not sleep for several nights after having inspected the human slaughterhouses of Odessa.

Such was the devilish fury and utter terror of those early years. In the nature of the case the Christian church, particularly in the persons of its leaders, tasted a special measure of this brutality. Of those who were not killed outright, many were dragged off into slave labor camps, where multitudes perished in the most pitiful circumstances.

Stalin's era was not known for its moderation and humanity. But even in the most recent times the persecution of Christians has been pursued vigorously in Russia. Quite recently people have been imprisoned for teaching the Christian faith to children. *Znamya Yunosti* (Emblem of Youth), an official Soviet publication, in its issue of March 29, 1967, tells of Mrs. Antonina Sitsh, whose son was taken away from her and placed in an atheistic orphanage by court order, because she had taught him to witness for Christ and keep his eyes shut during atheistic propaganda films in school. *Komsomolskaya Pravda* (Communist Youth League Truth) for May 22, 1966, isn't satisfied that 9-year old Kolya Sviridov has recanted properly: because of his Christian piety he had been placed into an atheistic boarding school. Since he continued to pray, he was handed over to Captain Hutorin of the secret police. This beast made him repeat: "There are no gods." The journal fears that Kolya may have meant only that the pagan, mythological gods do not exist! When his mother was allowed to see him, the boy asked: "Who is that woman?" What hell that little soul must have suffered already! *Doshkolnoye Vospitanie* (Pre-School Education) of March, 1966, shows a picture of the secret police seizing four children who are praying. They will be "re-educated" away from the "poison" of the Bible!

If such things are openly reported in official publications, it is not difficult to imagine the unpublished barbarities that must go on!

Naturally things are not very different in the other captive nations. Robert E.A. Lee's Question 7, based on the film which in turn was based on actual incidents and documents, is a penetrating study of persecution in East Germany. The story shows to what terrible pressures, particularly Christian youth are subjected. Subtlety, chicanery, and blackmail characterize the method in this case; it would be a mistake to conclude, however, that naked terror is not practiced in Stalinist East Germany.

Hungary is of particular interest because of the celebrated case of Cardinal Mindzenty. The cinematic interpretation of this affair in The Prisoner, never seemed quite convincing, despite Sir Alec Guinness' superb performance. Only our couch-obsessed culture could have suggested that mere talk broke the Cardinal. The real facts were very different. Not only was the Cardinal tortured unspeakably, but he was also subjected to the ultimate in scientific Satanism: the "Magic Room" described from experience, by Lajos Ruff in The Brain-Washing Machine. This treatment is reserved for those tough minds which cannot be broken by the methods of ordinary brutality. In this "Magic Room" a person can be equipped, by means of drugs, repetitious films and other "visual aids" and hypnotic suggestions, with an artificial memory. The victim can be made to "remember" quite sincerely crimes which he has never committed. These are then confessed in open court, when the prisoner is ready. If the subject survives, and does not become insane, the effect wears off after a time.

Probably the most valuable testimony that has recently come to light is that of Pastor Richard Wurmbrand, a converted Jew who became a Lutheran pastor in Romania, and languished in Communist prisons for fourteen years. He describes Christian clergymen and laymen being crucified and subjected to unmentionable torments. In his own body Pastor Wurmbrand bears deep marks of torture. For a long time he was kept in solitary confinement in a deep underground cell, without any light.

> No pains were spared to break him down. "It was an image of hell in which the suffering is eternal, but you cannot die. I was not the worst tortured, for here I am, alive. Nearly all our [Roman] Catholic bishops have been so handled that they died."
>
> Wurmbrand was flogged, forcibly filled up with water until his stomach swelled, then kicked around the room, bastinadoed while trussed like a chicken on a spit and submitted to other old and new devices in the interrogator's armory. A doctor was present at each session to see that he (as a valuable prisoner) did not die.[2]

One Roman Catholic priest had been forced to say Mass over urine and excrement. "Do not blame me," he begged. "I have suffered more than Christ!"

II. Persecution: A Study in Breadth

Before the Revolution the Russian Orthodox Church numbered 70 dioceses, 130 bishops, 50,960 priests, 94,629 monks and nuns and over 100,000,000 faithful. In the early sixties the figures released by the Moscow Patriarchate claimed 30,000 priests and 20,000 parishes, under the jurisdiction of 73 bishops. There were 67 convents and monasteries with an unknown number of monks and nuns.

One cannot simply subtract these later figures from the earlier ones. They represent different generations. Practically the entire hierarchy was eliminated in the twenties.

One should not overlook also typical situations like this one: Before the Revolution Moscow, with a population of 750,000, had over 2000 churches. Today, with a population of 7,000,000 only 20 churches are open. And if it were not for Moscow's function as a show-case for foreign visitors, not many of these would be open either:

The number of bishops, priests, and laymen who were liquidated cannot be statistically ascertained. Up to 1923 about 28 bishops and well over 1,200 priests had been murdered; many others had been deported, forced from their parishes or driven underground. Toward the end of 1927 a total of 117 bishops were listed as imprisoned or banished, in the years from 1929 to 1931 the attacks against the clergy gained new momentum during the troubles attending the collectivization of peasants. In 1934 four bishops were shot. According to Roman Catholic estimates a total of about 42,000 priests and bishops had been eliminated by the beginning of 1936. This figure included all those who had been executed, imprisoned, or put into concentration camps.[3]

The Roman Catholic Church in Russia numbered about 6,000,000 in 1917. Its organization was completely destroyed by the Reds.

In the archdiocese of Mohilev with the diocese of Minsk, where there had been 470 priests and 331 churches in 1917, only 16 priests and 30 churches were left in 1932. Of the 200 priests in the diocese of Shitomir there remained only six. In the year 1958 there was no hierarchy left in all of Byelorussia and only very few priests . . . in 1938, according to a compilation made by the Jesuit G.M. Schweigel, former professor at the Byelorussian College, there were only 500,000 [Roman] Catholics in Russia proper.[4]

About 8 million Roman Catholics came under direct Soviet rule in World War II. Take Lithuania as an example:

At the end of 1946, 350 priests were liquidated and several bishops were arrested and disappeared without a trace. By the beginning of 1949 about 600,000 Roman Catholics had been deported from Lithuania alone. During the first few months of 1950, 61 [Roman] Catholic priests and members of religious orders, among them two bishops and 18 prelates, were arrested, as it was announced, "at the urgent desire of a great number of the population" and were charged with espionage, sabotage, and malicious propaganda.

A large percentage of the 2,100,000 Germans who lived in Russia in 1917 were Lutherans, the Lutheran Church at that time had 539 parishes, with 1,828 churches and 230 pastors:

Her organization was destroyed without a trace. The churches were turned into movie houses, clubs, party centers, and stables.[6]

More than 100,000 Volga Germans perished during the civil war and the great famine. In the autumn and winter of 1929 many more were dragged off to Siberia as "kulaks"(prosperous farmers), where most of them died owing to the terrible conditions. Of the Black Sea Germans (224,000 Lutherans. 195,000 Roman Catholics, 104,000 Mennonites, prior to World War I) practically the whole male population was arrested during the purges of 1937 and 1938. When Hitler attacked the Soviet

Union in 1941, most of the male Volga Germans were sent to concentration camps or shot outright.

The largely Lutheran populations of Estonia and Latvia, annexed by the Soviet Union in 1940, were subjected to whole deportations. But the people were strongly attached to the Church, particularly in Estonia. In 1940 there had been about 2 million Lutherans in Estonia and Latvia. By 1957, after all the terror of the Stalin years, the Estonian Church still numbered 350,000 active members, while the Latvian Church counted 600,000 faithful.

There is no need to detail the statistics for the rest of Communist-held Europe. Enough has been said to enable us to form a fairly accurate picture of the overall situation. It is clear that the Christian Church behind the Iron Curtain is facing a persecution unparalleled in scope, intensity, and efficiency by anything in pagan antiquity. For the sake particularly of the valuable documentary references, I must add a few paragraphs about China:

> *The Red Book of the Persecuted Church* by John Gaiter, Newman Press, 1957, quotes *China Missionary Bulletin,* 1948, as giving the names and details of "more than 100 priests who were put to death often under *the most inhuman conditions" between 1947 and 1948 alone. The Systematic Destruction of the Catholic Church in China* by Thomas Bauer, World Horizons Reports, New York, 1954, states: "In the eight years from 1946 to 1954 a total of 166 members of the secular clergy and Religious Orders, both male and female, Chinese and foreign, have been executed by the government or had died of mistreatment in prison at the hands of their jailers." This report then appends the names and details of their deaths at the hands of the Communists.
>
> In addition there are a dozen or more books by Edward Hunter, Liu Shaw-tong, Rigney, Winance, Robert W. Greene, Dr. Paul K.T. Sih, Mark Tennien, De Jaegher, and Chow Ching-wen, to mention only a few, which cite cases and name names of Christian clergy and medical missionaries tortured and murdered by the Chinese Reds.
>
> Greta Palmer's "God's Underground in Asia" (Appleton-Century-Crofts, 1953) is devoted entirely to recounting the murders of religious workers, [Roman] Catholic and Protestant, by the Chinese Communists and the murderous persecution of the church in China. Hunter's *Black Book on Red China* (Bookmaller, New York, 1958) devotes a whole chapter to "Martyred Religion". Olin Stockwell's *With God in Red China* (Harper Brothers, New York, 1953) is sub-titled "What is happening to Christians in China".
>
> Last but not least in importance, is the testimony by several Protestant Chinese clergymen before the House Committee on Un-American Activities in March, 1959, and released as "Communist Persecution of Churches in Red China and Korea."

III. Communist "Law"

After the Revolution the new Red rulers at once confiscated all church property, and separated the schools from the Church. By a decree of January 23, 1918, the Council of People's Commissars guaranteed freedom of "cultic activities" (par. 5), so long as these did not interfere with the maintenance of public order. Par. 9 of the same decree, however forbade religious instruction in schools, while part. 12 deprived churches of their corporate character and forbade them to own property.

On April 8, 1929, all previous anti-religious legislation was summarized in the *Law Concerning Religion*, here are some of its provisions: Membership in religious societies is restricted to persons who have completed their eighteenth year (par. 3).

Religious societies are forbidden:

a) To collect funds for mutual assistance . . . and to use the property which is at their disposal for any purposes other than the satisfaction of their religious needs;

b) To grant material assistance to their members;

c) To organize prayer meetings and the like for children, youth or women; also meetings, groups, circles, sections devoted to the study of the Bible; . . . to establish children's playgrounds, libraries, or reading rooms; to organize sanatoriums and hospitals. In prayer rooms and buildings only such books may be kept as are necessary for the carrying on of the exercises of the religious cult in question (par. 17).

The field of activity of the ministers of religion, preachers, teachers, etc., is limited to the place of residence of the members of the religious society whom they are serving, and the place of their respective prayer houses (par. 19).

The exercise of religious rites and ceremonies and the keeping of religious objects are not permitted in institutions and buildings of the state, and in any public, co-operative, or private place (except for rooms that have been especially set aside at the request of a dying or seriously ill patient confined to a hospital and penal institution, and cemeteries and crematoria; here at least cultic exercises may take place). (par. 58).

Stalin's new Constitution of 1936 contained this Paragraph 124:

In order to assure to its citizens freedom of conscience the church in the U.S.S.R. is separated from the state, and the school is separated from the church, freedom in the exercise of a religious cult and of the freedom for antireligious propaganda is guaranteed to all citizens.

Religion here is limited to "The exercise of a religious cult", i.e. liturgical observances. Evangelism, Christian education, Christian charitable endeavors, and freedom to publish, as usually understood, are not covered by the term "religious cult", and are therefore forbidden. At the same time, the right to conduct anti-religious "propaganda" is explicitly safeguarded! This is the Orwellian "equality", where "some are more equal than others"!

It is true that the property disability, for instance, was removed during World War II, in gratitude for the services rendered by the Russian Orthodox Church. The policy change was merely tactical, however, and implied no abandonment by the Party, or its agent, the Soviet State, of the ultimate goal of the complete destruction of religion.

After Stalin's death it was even found necessary to tighten the existing anti-church legislation further. The November, 1962, number of *Sovetskaya lustitsia* (Soviet Justice), the official organ of the Ministry of Justice and of the Supreme Court of the Russian Soviet Federated Socialist Republic, announced a new law which:

> fixes the responsibility, the guilt, and the punishment for drawing into a religious group an underage, minor child. The . . . guilty ones may be the parents as well as any other member of the family or other person who invites any underage, minor child to attend a religious function. The punishment for the violation of the first part of Statute 227 of the Criminal Code of the R.S.F.S.R. is five years imprisonment or five years of exile.

The Soviet State does not mind old women gathering around ancient litanies, but is enraged at the thought of children and youth being won for Christ, or worse yet, learning how to win others. This cannot be tolerated. The recent Russian press is full of warning examples and exhortations about children being taken away from their parents on account of religious instruction, secret Sunday schools being discovered and their teachers convicted, and so on. Pastor Wurmbrand has described the situation very aptly: "Oh, religion is free, but you are not allowed to break; the law. And the law says that you are not allowed to spread religion"![8]

Article 124 of the Soviet Constitution is as much a fraud today as when Roosevelt used it to "prove" to America that Soviet principles of religious freedom were "essentially what is the rule in this country; only we don't put it quite the same way."[9] Averell Harriman was sent to Russia to obtain some official assurances in this regard, with which to placate American public opinion in view of the gigantic giveaway program which was then being prepared for Russia's benefit, at the expense of the American tax-payer. In due course Harriman received the official assurance "that the Soviets did allow religious worship and would reduce restrictions and would have the necessary publicity." Harriman's own confidential appraisal was not of course made public till much later; "in spite of all comments and assurances, I leave with the impression that all the Soviets intend to do is to give lip service and to create certain instances which would give an impression of relaxation without really changing their present practices."[10]

The wild, bloody terror of the early years is gone, to be sure. But oppression and anti-religious propaganda continue. The ineffectiveness of these methods was demonstrated already in the 1937 census, when the question about religion, intended to demonstrate the death of Christianity, revealed 50,000,000 believers. This was so embarrassing that the returns were scrapped and the census officials arrested.[11] No religious information was sought in the 1939 and 1959 censuses.

There are in fact voices in the Communist empire, which seem to have learned from the West that material prosperity and indifference are far more effective weapons against religion than active persecution. The Polish Communist Taddeusz Pluzanski has written:

61

To force atheism upon the people will lead only to a strengthening of piety. Poland cannot be secularized through the efforts of atheists and freethinkers . . . Direct anti-religious propaganda creates unrest and does not help secularization but retards it because it provokes the opposition of the faithful . . . Religion whose present revival is merely the logical result of Stalin's oppression, will decline again once normal conditions return to Poland. This cooling-off process in the religious area can be developed into a trend by isolating religious problems so that they will become a completely private concern, in an atmosphere of indifference religious fervor will disappear very quickly.[12]

And the Polish Minister of Education, Bienkowski, insisted:

Only by supporting indifference can we prepare the way for the decline of the influence of the church. The death of religion does not start with a fight against religion, but with the death of the problems which are favoring religion.[13]

IV. Rule, Ruin and Exploit: The Official Church

A few days before the Communist take-over, the All-Russian Synod, convoked by the Kerensky government, decided to restore the Russian Orthodox Patriarchate, which had been vacant since 1721, when Peter the Great abolished the office and transferred its functions to the Czars. As head of the Russian Church, Patriarch Tikhon excommunicated all "who had abused their high positions to persecute the church and the Christian people". That was in January, 1919. In September Tikhon decreed that the clergy should be completely neutral in politics. In 1922 Tikhon was arrested and imprisoned, his trial never took place, for on June 16, 1923, the Patriarch published an abject confession, in which he accused himself of having held negative attitudes toward the Soviet regime, but promised henceforth to refrain from all opposition, and to disavow all connections with anti-Communist forces. Thereupon he was released, but died in 1925.

The State did not allow the election of a new patriarch. The new leader of the Church, Metropolitan Sergius, after imprisonment, was recognized as "Administrator of the Church of Moscow." Sergius identified the interests of Church completely with those of the State, and made fulsome declarations of loyalty. For this reason he was opposed by the conservative bishops (a total of 80 between 1923 and 1926) interned on the island Solovki, in the White Sea. From now on the Soviet secret police entered the Church's governing body. Seeing that the Church was not so easily destroyed, the Communists decided at least to exploit it for their own purposes even while attempting to destroy it.

Those who opposed Sergius' compromises, were called the "Tikhon Church", and were bitterly persecuted. The "Sergius Church", the officially tolerated branch, was nicknamed "fall-down-and-worship-me" (Mat.4:9) by the people.

In World War II Stalin found it useful to replace Communist internationalism with fervent Russian patriotism. The subservient Church did its part to portray the war effort as a crusade on behalf of Holy Mother Russia. The fantastic sum of 300,000,000 rubies was raised by the Church, and used to present a fighter squadron, christened "Alexander Nevsky", and a tank column, named "Dmitri Donskoy", to the Red Army!

The Church's loyalty was rewarded in 1943, when Stalin elevated the Russian Orthodox Church to a privileged position, and allowed it to elect a new Patriarch at last.

The official publications of the Moscow Patriarchate spoke of Stalin in the most idolatrous terms, and followed whatever political line was demanded at the moment. The special government department created to deal with the Russian Church, was headed by G. Karpov, of the secret police. Russians who were in a position to know, have told me that the secret police would frequently appoint its own agents as bishops, that priests were trained merely to carry out the ritual and to preach propaganda, and that the people feared and despised the clergy of the "established" Church as agents of the regime.

At New Delhi, where the Moscow Patriarchate was received into membership of the World Council of Churches, the Russian churchmen lived in the Soviet Embassy, travelled in the Embassy limousine, and invited their fellow-delegates to a screening of Communist propaganda films at Travancore Hall, a part of the Soviet Embassy.

The Communists have found their ecclesiastical branch to be a very valuable tool for the spreading of "peace" propaganda among the churches and societies of the West.

The same policy has been pursued wherever possible also in the satellite nations. Thus the Hungarian Reformed bishop, Janos Peter, who had attended the 1954 assembly of the World Council of Churches in Evanston, U.S.A., and had extolled the religious freedom to be found under Communism, reappeared in the U.S.A. in 1959, this time as First Deputy Foreign Minister of Communist Hungary, in which capacity he brazenly justified before the U.N. the brutal suppression of the Hungarian Revolution of 1956!

The head of the Hungarian Reformed Church, Albert Bereczky, a former member of the Communist underground, was elected to the Central Committee of the World Council of Churches in 1955.

In Czechoslovakia there is the notorious Joseph L. Hromadka, another "ecumenical" figure, who has been identified as a Communist tool in Communist! Penetration into Australian churches, by former Czech Communist writer V.L. Borin. Dr. Michael Zibrin, a former member of the Parliament in Prague, and former Superintendent of the Lutheran Church in Slovakia, has named the head of that church, Chabada, as a Communist agent.

He also says:

A re-organization of the Lutheran Church had started - and what a reorganization! Faithful pastors were in every case imprisoned and ousted, and their offices were given to women with Communist Party cards. They had practically no schooling, no fitness for their work, no love of God, in fact no religion

63

at all. Their manners and behavior made a mockery of the church![14]

Pastor Richard Wurmbrand has testified that the Romanian Communists offered him immediate release from prison, re-union with his family, and the top church post in Romania, if he would agree to work for the regime. Pastor Wurmbrand agreed on the condition that he be supplied with a visiting card stating: "Rev. R. Wurmbrand, Bishop, secret police." He remained in prison. But not everyone had such strength of character!

The Chinese regime, as is well-known, was particularly harsh. A socialist cleric, Y.T. Wu, who incidentally had been trained at Union Seminary in New York, and had been a Vice President of the World Council of Churches, welcomed Communism with open arms, and even formulated the pledge which all church-leaders were required henceforth to give: "I pledge to guide the people under my care along the road to socialism under the direction of the Communist Party."

The Anglican Missionary Paul Denlinger reports:

> We began to get sermons in our local church about Jesus Christ being a great revolutionary and how he was interested in changing the world. Eventually, we got out-and-out Communism, not even cloaked in the Social Gospel. It got to be so hard to take that we could hardly say our prayers. . . The hierarchy of the church in China was completely discredited in the eyes of Chinese Christians . . . Any priest whom the people respected was under constant pressure from the regime, and under attack and criticism from the hierarchy of his own church. Seeing this, the lay Christians began to organize prayer groups in their own homes, ignoring the formal structure of the Church . . . Often the local minister, if he discovered his church members holding such meetings, would report them to the local Communist authorities.[16]

The "Three-Self" Movement, directed against all foreign involvements, even succeeded in detaching the Roman Catholic structure from the Pope. A loyal Roman Catholic complained to the German journalist Dr. Peter Schmidt, who had not noticed any outward changes when he attended Mass in Shanghai:

> We do not know whether they have signed the declaration of loyalty. Brainwashing is done very discreetly, and nobody notices anything of it. We have only one criterion by which we can recognize the truth. The true church today is very poor. On the altar there are a few miserable flowers. The lights are extinguished as soon as daylight makes it possible to see what is going on. Electricity is saved. We find out about the betrayal of our priests only through devious ways. When they have lots of flowers on the altar and when the lights are burning in the church in the daytime we know they have been unfaithful. For the devil is very much interested in giving to his own all these gifts with which the churches can be renovated externally and can be shown to the world as beautiful empty shells, as proof of how pious the Communists are.[17]

There are notable exceptions to the rule that the official church and its leaders are Communist tools. The Roman Catholic Church of Poland, for instance, under Cardinal Wyszynski, has succeeded in retaining its spiritual independence. And so has the Evangelical Church of East Germany. In Germany there was in fact at first a very cordial relationship between the new Communist regime and the ecclesiastical leadership, who had all suffered together in Nazi concentration camps, despite this early cordiality, a fearful struggle came to the surface in 1952. The state was determined to supplant Christian sacraments and rites like Baptism, Confirmation, and weddings, with pagan, Communist oriented observances, like "name-giving" ceremonies and "youth dedications". The oppression continues to this day. There are also individual exceptions like the Lutheran Bishop Lajos Ordass of Hungary, who was kept by the Communists practically under house arrest. As soon as the Red yoke had been cast off in 1956, Ordass was made head of the Lutheran Church of Hungary. But he was removed again when Communism was re-imposed by Soviet might.

In view of this situation two dangers must be avoided: on the one hand Western churchmen must be careful lest they offend and insult the suffering Church behind the Iron curtain by hobnobbing with its tormentors and their stooges. On the other hand, we must not be too quick to condemn individuals who may be forced to play a detestable role, but who believe that by yielding to the political demands of their captors, they are at least preserving some sort of legal existence and *modus vivendi* for the Church. Although I cannot agree with a number of Hutten's judgments, which seem too optimistic to me, it could be significant that, as he points out, even the most subservient Moscow Patriarchate in its *Journal* and other publications provides "no proof that Marxist ideology had ever taken root in the Church. In the historical articles published by the Church no mention was made that looked like a dialectical-materialistic interpretation of church history."[18]

V. The Triumph of the Resurrected: The Underground Church

In Communist countries where the official church apparatus has been to all intents and purposes captured, there exists also an underground Church. Its clergy go about secretly baptizing, instructing, confirming, evangelizing, and celebrating the Christian mysteries. The Soviet press indicates that the numbers involved must be considerable, and constitute a serious headache for the authorities.

A significant article appeared in the March, 1967 issue of the Canadian *Prairie Overcomer*. It was Paul B. Peterson's "The Protestant Church in Russia Today". The author points out that there is considerable dissatisfaction with the leadership of the official "Union of Evangelical Christians-Baptists" whose head, Zhidkov, is regarded as a tool of the Reds. Peterson reports tremendous spiritual vigor, mass baptisms, also of Communist youth, etc., on the part of the unofficial Evangelical movement. These groups have grown so strong that they have pressed the government for recognition as independent bodies. Thus on May 16, 1966 there arrived in Moscow a delegation of 500 evangelical Christians, who wished to petition the government for the right to form their own organization. They refused to disperse, and were finally imprisoned. But the work continues to grow.

Pastor Wurmbrand, who also points out that the show-case Moscow "Baptist" Church is in fact a State-maintained merger of all sorts of Protestant denominations, claims that the underground Church infiltrates not only the official Church, but even the very secret police itself!

Great suffering is endured with much heroism by this underground Church. One of its Romanian pastors refused to divulge any names under torture. Then the pastor's fourteen year old son was brought in, and the inquisitors undressed him and began to beat him savagely before the eyes of the horrified father, who then broke down and offered to tell all they wished to know. But the heroic boy cried, "Father, if I die, my last words will be 'Jesus and my fatherland'. I can die for them. But don't betray!"

Here is another remarkable instance from the experience of Pastor Wurmbrand: One day the prisoners were amazed to find one of their main tormentors thrown into the cell with them. He told them his story. A twelve-year old boy had brought him some flowers and said: "Today is my mother's birthday, and on her birthday I always gave her flowers, but now I no longer have a mother, because you have killed her. But I know that she would be happy if I loved my enemies. Therefore, comrade, will you please take these flowers home to your wife!" The hardened Communist was so stunned that he could not persecute any more Christians, and so was thrown into prison together with them, and became one of them!

The following case is documented in *Murder International, Inc.,* released by the Internal Security Sub-Committee of the U.S. Senate.

Yanina Khokhlov, 32, a skilled construction engineer and a devout Christian, was married to Nikolai Khokhlov, an officer of the Soviet government's assassination squad ("Department of wet affairs"), which specializes in liquidating inconvenient anti-Communists abroad. Through his wife's efforts, Nikolai had become a Christian too, and their baby had been secretly baptized. When ordered to assassinate a prominent anti-Communist in West Germany, the Khokhlovs formed a plan to escape. Because of his Christian faith he gave himself up to the very man he was supposed to kill. His wife and baby were to follow him to the West, but were caught by the secret police and sent to Siberia. This happened in 1954. Such Christians can pray from experience those terrible lines in Luther's "A Mighty Fortress":

And take they our life
Goods, fame, child and wife
Though these all be gone
Yet have our foes not won
The Kingdom ours remaineth!

The fact is that there is a vast spiritual hunger in the Communist world. Men and women of all walks of life are looking for that which the Christian church has to offer.

David Benson reports that while he was working in Moscow, he was approached by a biochemist who asked him various thoughtful questions about God, and complained that Soviet life offered no opportunity to dis cuss such questions. A few days later a young woman approached me and began to speak in very broken English . . . "I am an atomic physicist here in Russia," she said, "and I want to ask, do you think the structure of the atom shows signs of a Mind that made it?"

When I replied that I did, this woman broke into tears. "So do I," she sobbed. "There must be a God! There must be a God!"[9]

Bibles sell in Russia for the equivalent of 40 to 50 Australian dollars! John Noble, who spent some years in the slave-labor camp at Vorkuta, beyond the Arctic Circle, reports that "the Church behind barbed wire" is nourishing, and that even hardened communist camp commanders secretly study the Bible, because they are amazed at the evident power of its message.

I report these details because there exists a wide-spread fallacy to the effect that Christianity is a tender plant which needs the protection of Western military might to survive. That is not true. The religion of Christ has its own supernatural power and protection, by virtue of which it triumphs in the midst of its enemies!

VI. Toward A Christian Perspective

1. The Christian regards history not as a meaningless series of contingent situations accidentally turning out this way or that, but as the scaffolding within which a personal God is pursuing His purposes, and that nothing happens or can happen without His directive or permissive will.

2. Communism therefore is not a random historical development, but a judgment of God, which will be taken away only when it has accomplished those purposes for which God has permitted it to arise. No one who is at all familiar with the history of European Christianity in the last few centuries, with the corruption, worldliness, and superstition on the one hand, and the dogmatic dissolution and secularization on the other, can doubt that the terrible scourge of Communism is just and well-deserved.

3. But we cannot repent for other people. We must look to our own spiritual lives, and to our own churches. Is our religion more than a venerable tradition? Do we care which of several conflicting alternatives is the true teaching of the New Testament? Do we care whether our church adheres to it? Are we zealous for the sacred work Christ has given to His Church? Do we have the courage to confess our commitment to Him, and the interest to learn His teaching - as intensely as Marxists study and practice Marxism? The living martyrs under Communist persecution do not want or need our pity. But we desperately need to be inspired by their faith and devotion, and to honor them by following their example.

4. As Christian citizens and subjects, we also have obligations to our nation. One of these is to defend our neighbor and our country against all who seek to harm them. Here we must know what God has given the State the right to use force in the projection of law and order. We shall therefore not join the general whining for compromise and surrender, but on the contrary, tear the Christian mask off the unholy business of exploiting Christian feelings in the interests of an inhuman, atheistic con-

spiracy. Martin Luther, for instance, often pointed out that it was a duty to fight the Turks, who were at that time threatening Europe. Our modern "Turks", threatening all civilization, are of course the Communists.

5. At the same time we will not confuse *any* political cause with that of Christ. His Kingdom is not of this world. This Kingdom can be neither defended nor destroyed by the sword. Church and State each have their appropriate functions and methods. While the Church is ruled by Christ through the written, supernatural revelation of His Word, the State must be governed according to the light of reason, and of natural law. This means that anti-Communism should not be presented as something distinctly or specifically Christian. No political program or action as such can be "Christian". What can be Christian or not is the *motivation*. Non-Christians can be anti-Communists for reasons of self-defense, defense of vested interests, patriotism, ideology, etc. Christians must be anti-Communists not from any selfish considerations, but as part of their total service to Christ, Who has commanded us to honor lawful authorities and to seek and promote our neighbors' welfare.

6. Finally, while the Christian as a citizen will hate and fight any atheistic, materialistic world-view, and will strongly advocate and support all necessary measures, including military force, to defeat the international Communist conspiracy, to thwart its schemes in his own country, and to promote the liberation of countries now enslaved, he may not as a Christian, hate his enemies as individuals, but must ever love them and pray for them, even in the midst of bitter conflict!

FOOTNOTES

1. R. Nilostonski, *Der Blutrausch des Bolschewismus* (The Blood-Lust of Bolshevism).
2. Chades Foley, "The Man From God's Underground", *National Review,* Vol. XX, No.8 (February
   27, 1968), P. 184.
3. Kurt Hutten, *Iron Curtain Christians* (Minneapolis: Augsburg, 1967), p. 11.
4. ibid., p. 65
5. ibid., p. 66
6. ibid., p. 68
7. Quoted in Major E. Bundy, "The 'Expert' Epidemic". *News and Views*, September, 1962.
8. "The New Communist Propaganda Line on Religion", Hearing before the Committee on Un-American Activities, House of Representatives, (U.S.A), Ninetieth Congress, First Session, August 10, 1967, p. 530.
9. Quoted in George N. Crocker, *Roosevelt's Road to Russia* (Chicago: Henry Regnery, 1959) p. 146.
10. ibid., p. 148.
11. Walter Kolarz, *Religion in the Soviet Union* (London: Macmillan, 1961), p. 12.
12. K. Hutten, op. cit., pp. 102-103.
13. ibid.
14. Quoted in *Lutheran News* (New Haven, Mo., U.S.A.), Sept. 23, 1963, p. 7
15. William G. Goddard, *The Story of Chang Lao* (Melbourne: Australian League of Rights, 1962), pp. 61-62
16. Paul B. Denlinger, "The Christian Church and the Communists in China", *Intelligence Survey*. August, 1963, pp. 4-5
17. K. Hutten, op. cit., p. 441.
18. ibid., p. 26.
19. David V. Benson, *Christianity, Communism, and Survival* (Glendale, Calif., Regal,

68

QUESTION: *Do you see any other alternative for our nation, other than to go through the horrors you have described, "Through hell to Heaven"?*

ANSWER: I hope and pray that there is, but I am not a prophet. Objectively, and humanly speaking, I have no doubt that the West could win, if it had the will but it is our will which is being broken down.

It terrifies me to see such a large part of the electorate seemingly concerned only about maximum wages and minimum beer prices, and not at all about national security, which is the paramount issue. It should be unthinkable, as national suicide, to elect to public office anyone even remotely connected with Communist or pro-Communist forces. Yet such elements do get into office.

Then people say naively: "O well, there's only a handful of Communists in Australia!"

Fred Schwarz answers that one very well with the analogy of the ship that has sprung a leak: There may be very little water in the ship so far, but the danger lies in its connection with a great deal of water outside! Nor will it do to say: "But look how much of the ship's surface is still intact!" The Communist apparatus may lie numerically small in this country, but it must be measured in terms of the total power of the world-wide Communist conspiracy, whose agent it is.

QUESTION: *I understand you to say that Communism is a judgment of God upon the world and would be removed when it had accomplished its purpose. But how do you answer the argument, which I have had put to me, that to fight against Communism is to fight against the will and judgment of God?*

ANSWER: We must, as Christians, be guided by the revealed will of God, and not speculate about His hidden will. If gangsters attack my neighbor and his family, it is my duty to come to their defense. It is not my duty to speculate whether it may not perhaps be God's will to punish or discipline my neighbors through some tragedy. That may be His will, but I cannot assume it. My job is to do the best I can to protect and defend them. I may have to go down fighting, but it is better to have fought and lost, than never to have fought at all. It is the same with Communism. If, having done all to protect my neighbors against this plague, it should prevail, I would accept it as a divine judgment - and begin at once to pray and look for deliverance. Meanwhile my business is not to speculate about God's inscrutable purposes in particular historical situations, but to do the best I can for the welfare of my fellow human beings.

What really erodes our national will and courage is not the Christian Faith, but secular Liberalism, oozing out of the universities. Malcolm Muggeridge recently called this philosophy "a collective death-wish". Our intellectuals, or at least a large and vocal body of them, do not believe in "our side". They want "us" to lose. They can't wait for the total crumbling of the remnants of "Christian civilization", with all its virtues and vices. While a culture can normally look to its intellectuals to sustain, explain, defend, and extend it, many of our intellectuals are betraying us in this regard. They despise our religious and cultural heritage, and can't wait to replace it with some form of rationalist-humanist-materialist ideology. This of course plays into the hands of the Marxists, who regard our universities as rich fields ripe unto harvest!

You can observe the "collective death-wish" in action almost anywhere; on T.V. in pompous A.B.C. commentators, in *The Australian* editorials, etc. For example: everything the black races in Africa do, even when they murder each other and whites, is excused and forgotten. But when the civilized government of Rhodesia executes convicted murderers and petrol-bombers, the whole artificial mass-media world screams as if, as Bill Buckley observed, the Rhodesians "had just finished executing Florence Nightingale, her mother, and her father!" You see the topsy-turvy sense of values: anything the enemy does is at least understandable; but our side is wicked and corrupt! Vietnam is treated that way too.

The case for Western Civilization needs to be put much more convincingly in our universities!

QUESTION: *Would it be possible to obtain a prayer list for people who are suffering under Communism?*

ANSWER: I think the best thing to do would be to write to Mission to Europe's Millions, P.O. Box 11, Glendale, Calif., U.S.A., through which Pastor Wurmbrand works. I agree with his statement that "No Christian Liturgy is valid without a prayer for the martyrs!"

QUESTION: *Could you outline some sources of strength for this struggle? Could the World Council of Churches, perhaps, be of help here in uniting Christians for joint resistance to Communism?*

ANSWER: This is a ticklish question, and I wish I could honestly say, "Yes". I would not like to offend anyone, but I must give my honest conviction, I am unable to regard the World Counsel of Churches as very helpful, and that for two reasons, one theological, the other political.

In the first place, The World Council seems to be trying simply to collect as many people and organizations as possible under one organizational roof, without any regard for real spiritual unity on the basis of truth. But Christian unity must rest on obedience to Christ's Word, not on numbers or big-ness. The Church is a spiritual organism, not a super-organization. It is found not by sight, but by faith, and only where Christ is found, namely in His Gospel and Sacraments. To compromise these, for the sake of big-ness and a "united front", is not to strengthen, but to weaken the Church. It destroys, and does not advance real, God-pleasing unity.

On a more mundane level, the World Council seems to be even more of a liability. Many leading Western churchmen, having been educated at seminaries where historic Christianity was "out", and Darwinism, Social Gospel, etc., "in", are ideologically predisposed toward Marxism, and are exploited accordingly. Some are even conscious Marxists. There was the notorious case of Harry Ward, who taught at Union Seminary for about 40 years, and was a Communist all along. This one man has had

70

tremendous influence, not only directly, through the social creed he worked out for the entire Federal Council of Churches, as it was then called, but indirectly through thousands of his students, many of whom are now in leading positions.

The World Council is being used as a forum for Communist attacks on the West, but rarely does it work the other way around. Read the New Delhi Report. The pro-Communist bias, of for instance, the actual recommendations of the W.C.C.'s Commission of the Churches for international Affairs (C.C.I.A.) is quite startling. And last year's conference under W.C.C. auspices, in Geneva, on Christianity and Revolution was blatantly Marxist. It was thought to be the Church's job to promote world revolution and hasten the universal advent of some form of Marxism!

For spiritual strength and guidance, I would have to look in very different directions. Divine revelation, not human revolution must inform Christian convictions!

Christian News, October 7, 1968

1. Kurt Marquart was born in ____.
2. It is difficult for those who have not directly experienced Communism to ____.
3. How were Christian clergy often tormented? ____.
4. The Red counter-revolution replaced ____.
5. Who experienced a special measure of brutality? ____.
6. What did the film Question 7 portray? ____.
7. What happened to Cardinal Mindzenty? ____.
8. What did Richard Wurmbrand experience? ____.
9. According to Roman Catholic estimates, how many priests and bishops had been eliminated by 1936? ____.
10. What happened to the Lutheran Church in Russia? ____.
11. Where were most of the Volga Germans sent? ____.
12. What happened to the Christian Church in China? ____.
13. Membership is religious societies was restricted to ____.
14. The ultimate goal of the Communist Party was ____.
15. The Soviet State is enraged at ____.
16. Franklin Roosevelt used the Soviet Constitution to prove ____.
17. Patriarch Tikhon published ____.
18. The Soviet secret police entered ____.
19. How did the publications of the Moscow Patriarchs refer to Stalin? ____.
20. What did Bishop Janos Peter justify? ____.
21. Joseph L. Hromadka was identified as ____.
22. Where was Y. T. Wu trained? ____.
23. In Germany Christian sacraments were supplanted by ____.
24. Zhidkov was regarded as ____.
25. How does the Christian regard history ____.
26. Our modern "Turks" threatening all civilization are ____.
27. Christians should ____ for their enemies?
28. Christian convictions must be informed by ____.

71

LICKING HEROD'S BLOODY BOOTS

Evangelical Catechism or Ecumenical Cataclysm?
(The Six Chief Parts vs. ALC/LWF/WCC)

(FOURTH IN A SERIES)

THE FOURTH AND FIFTH COMMANDMENTS:

Thou shall honor thy father and thy mother, that it may be well with thee and thou mayest live long upon the earth.

Thou shalt not kill.

Lutherans have generally understood the Augsburg Confession's teaching that Christianity is not some revolutionary social agitation:

"The Gospel does not overthrow civil authority, the state, and marriage but requires that all these be kept as true orders of God and that everyone, each according to his own calling, manifest Christian love and genuine good works in his station of life. Accordingly Christians are obliged to be subject to civil authority and obey its commands and laws in all that can be done without sin. But when commands of the civil authority cannot be obeyed without sin, we must obey God rather than men (Acts 5:29)" (Art. XVI , 5-7).

No doubt these are still basically the convictions of most rank and file members of the Lutheran Church-Missouri Synod. But the revolutionary propagandists have already gone to work on them even at the highest church-political level. Consider this insinuation from the notorious LCUSA booklet, "Who Can This Be?:

"Historically, Lutheran churches have aligned themselves more with the preservation of the status quo rather than with the forces which have sought liberation from dominating governmental structures. If existing structures seem to protect and strengthen the already rich, while the victims of poverty find their miserable lot intensified, how might a revolutionary gospel about a revolutionary Christ speak to the question of social and political change? What freedom is given to align oneself with rapid change when the concern is for the betterment of the lives of the poor and forgotten" (p. 35).

Here we have the totally anti-Christian "Theology of Revolution," as it was cooked up at the Geneva Conference on Church and Society in 1966 and ratified by the World Council of Churches at Uppsala in 1968. Meanwhile, the L.W.F. has got into the act too, with its approval, from

Geneva, of the use of violence. It would be futile to deny that many people swept up in this movement honestly believe that they are doing their Christian duty to the poor and downtrodden of this world. It would be equally futile to deny that many of these same people have lost all meaningful faith in the supernatural doctrines of Christianity. Having lost Heaven, they seek their paradise on earth— and ironically become the unwitting tools of the sinister which are building colonies of hell on earth!

Nobody changed the world more effectively than did the ancient Christians. Today's Christians bursting with zeal for social reform should ponder LIFE magazine's remarkably perceptive Easter editorial of April 19, 1954, about how the early Christians did it:

> "While creating Western Civilization, their minds were on something else . . . like corals building the Great Barrier Reef, all these Christians created our Western Civilization as the unplanned by-product of their personal hope and labor . . . If we really wish to defend and extend it . . . we can do so only by imitating the builders whose real hope was elsewhere. . . And the glory of the Christian hope is that it is not offered to 'the world' but to living men and women for a life beyond."

How Sincere?

Imagine St. Paul rabble-rousing among Roman slaves, and organizing demonstrations in front of Nero's palace for the abolition of slavery!

And how does it help the poor and underprivileged, when power-hungry terrorists, gangsters, and arsonists, black and white, are drooled over and glorified, so that they can blackmail the civilized community all the better? The poor gain nothing but new and more brutal masters, and the whole community stands to lose everything, if terrorism and mob-violence are condoned. Freedom and justice do not arise out of revolutionary terror, as the French and all Communist revolutions amply prove!

At this point we can test the sincerity of the LCUSA booklet's revolutionary Social Gospel, What about "liberation from dominating governmental structures"? Is this a plea to come to the aid of the millions of oppressed Christians behind the Iron Curtain? What more horribly "dominating governmental structures" are there in the world today than the Communist slave regimes? Are we to work for "rapid change . . . for the betterment of the lives of the poor and forgotten" behind the Iron Curtain?

The LCUSA editors would no doubt be horrified by any suggestion that they meant anything of this kind! Their jargon is borrowed from those whose twisted mentality (see Burnham's SUICIDE OF THE WEST) sees America as Public Enemy Number One!

If the LCUSA power-clique had a conscience about Communist oppression, they would have been able to secure respect for their views at the World Council of Churches assembly in Uppsala last year. But they didn't. Here is the impartial, Christian way in which Uppsala dispensed its favors, judgments, and anathemas:

It honored the fanatically anti-Christian and anti-American author of ANOTHER COUNTRY.

It honored the Communist propagandist, Pete Seeger, who sang "protest songs," but didn't of course protest the outstanding crimes of our times, the Communist mass-murders.

African Blood-Bath

It honored President Kenneth Kaunda of Zambia, who virtually called for a crusade against Angola, Rhodesia, and South Africa, and promised a blood-bath much worse than Vietnam unless Western civilization in Southern Africa meekly and unconditionally surrendered! (Interesting comparison: The Communists must build Iron Curtains and Berlin Walls to keep their subjects from getting OUT of the Workers' Paradise. Much-maligned South Africa has the problem of trying to stop the 50,000 "liberated" natives, some of them from Kaunda's Zambia, who every year get INTO the country, illegally, for the sake of a higher standard of living! Yet Soviet Russia must be constantly and abjectly begged for the favor of a detente, while it is our Christian duty to vilify South Africa at every opportunity).

At Uppsala the W.C.C. faced three International crisis:

(1) In Vietnam America was defending South Vietnam against Chinese and Russian-backed Communist invasion, aggression and terrorism.

(2) In Biafra, the Christian Ibos were faced with what some observers believed to be genocide on the part of federal Nigerian troops, many of them-Moslems. Ancient tribal hatreds were involved too.

(3) Soviet Russia was massing troops on the borders of Czechoslovakia, in order to re-impose rigid, oppressive Marxism on the people, who had finally succeeded in struggling free from some of its strangling tentacles.

How did the "Christian summit" at Uppsala react to these situations?

(1) It condemned America's intervention in Vietnam. The first speaker on the subject, Dean Lonning of the Bergen Cathedral (Norway), objected to the one-sided condemnation of the U.S.A., and moved an amendment so that the reference would be to "the intervention of great powers." This was warmly applauded from the floor. But the General Secretary, Eugene Carson Blake, intervened to rule that this amendment had to be tabled until everybody had had a chance to speak to the original, unamended motion! Even so, the next two speakers, a Filipino and a Japanese, also objected to the resolution, on the grounds that it was contrary to historical fact and that it took no notice of the murderous Viet Cong attacks on South Vietnamese civilians.

In the end, after prominent American delegates had cravenly begged for a condemnation, the weary delegates passed the original, blatantly unfair and unjust resolution!

74

(2) Biafra could not even be referred to as such, since the Nigerian delegates would then have walked out—-and after all that would at once have destroyed the Ecumenical nature of the assembly! So Biafra became "the former eastern region" in an insipid "peace" resolution whose one solitary tooth, a clause calling upon the nations of the world to stop supplying arms to the belligerents, was first carefully extracted! (Britain and Soviet Russia are supplying arms to Nigeria. It might have been feasible to condemn a wicked colonial power like Britain, but, oh dear, the peace-loving Soviet Union–well that was another matter!)

Calling Evil Good and Good Evil

(3) Nothing at all was said *about* Czechoslovakia, where "unilateral intervention of a great power" was imminent. The W.C.C. dare not criticize Communism in any way, lest all the "representatives" of the fictitious "free churches" of the Socialist Commonwealth, be withdrawn at once, together with their chaperons of the secret police. And that would be such an unthinkable loss to peace on earth and goodwill toward men!

The upshot of this whole hypocritical farce is a Satanic perversion of Christian ethics: Civic righteousness must be denounced as sinful and criminal while real crimes and brutalities must be covered up and ignored. The American defense of the South Vietnamese people against enslavement by the detested Communist butchers is immoral, but violence and terrorism against the governments and private citizens of South Africa, Rhodesia, and the U.S.A., is a legitimate struggle for "liberation from dominating governmental structures." To those gangsters who seek to plunge our whole society, including its large and prosperous working Class, into a blood-bath of terror and civil war, we are supposed to say, with "Father" Groppi; "Black Power! Don't get caught, Joe!" Arson, looting, injury, abuse, even killing are merely "rapid change" it seems, all "for the betterment of the lives of the poor and forgotten"! Meanwhile the real poor and forgotten—the slaves behind the Iron Curtain—remain poor and forgotten! Criminals are Good and police are Bad. Law and order in America are an un-Christian, unbearable oppression, destined for "rapid change"; but the real tyranny and barbarity of Communism is good. Christian peace, and anyone who suggests "rapid change" there must be an irresponsible warmonger!

If that is Christianity, then Herod, not Jesus, is the Christ!

The Jews have not ceased to this day to remind the world through the mass media, again and again, of the six millions Jews murdered by Hitler. But the World Council of Churches feels no comparable loyalty to the millions of Christians killed and tortured to this day under Communism! In fact the W.C.C. s officials seem more at ease hobnobbing with the persecutors than with the persecuted!

When Israeli agents kidnapped Eichmann from a foreign country, everyone purred with satisfaction. But what if American C.I.A. agents were to kidnap Khrushchev, and bring him to trial in New York for his Ukrainian blood-bath? The unctuous peace-and love politicians of the World Council would be the first to howl self-righteous denunciations!

If the Ecumenical Movement cannot do anything to help the captive Christians under Communist persecution, then at least it should not lie about them, and pretend to the world that black is white!

Church Press Lied About Czechoslovakia

Prof. Dr. A. Hudak, of Erlangen University, has written in the Dec. 1968 issue of the KORRESPONDENZBLATT, published by the "Pfarreverein" (organization of pastors) of the Lutheran State Church of Bavaria:

(After several paragraphs of concrete evidence of Communist persecution of the Church in Czechoslovakia, taken from official ecclesiastical documents during Prague's few precious weeks of relative freedom. Prof. Hudak continues:)

"He who, five or ten years ago, said or wrote among us the very same things which during the brief time of the Prague 'thaw' the churches there themselves said, was dismissed among us as an 'intractable anticommunist crusader'. On our side it was being written: For the Christians in Czechoslovakia the new social structure means a genuine perspective for the future. But the General Council of the Evangelical Lutheran Church in Slovakia declared: The believers were driven into 'moral isolation' in this new social structure. On our side it was said by the highest ecclesiastical authority: There is no persecution of churches in the Eastern states. But now we hear—in the time of the Prague 'thaw'—of incarcerated pastors and congregational members . . .

"The very Church which bows down in deepest reverence before the pluralism of our social structure, knew no pluralistic reporting of facts with reference to the situation of the Church in the East, in large sections of our ecclesiastical press. He who still dared to say or write anything different here, was pushed into a corner.

"One can perhaps understand that in view of church politics and Ecumenical interests this and that could not be said or written too loudly. But such considerations must find their limits, also in the ecclesiastical press, where the truth is at stake. 'We can do nothing against the truth, but for the truth.' Therefore we must maintain: The self-portrait of the Church In Czechoslovakia, painted at the time of the Prague 'thaw', radically contradicts the picture which our ecclesiastical press has been drawing for us in the past 15 years about the situation of the Church in Czechoslovakia."

Underground Church

World Council leaders claim to believe that their policies toward Soviet-controlled churches are necessary in order to keep in touch with, and strengthen the Christians behind the Iron Curtain. In relation to the real facts, these threadbare excuses sound sickeningly cynical. Official recognition and honoring of their slave-masters' and tormentors' stooges and puppets does not help the captive Christians! It merely adds bitter insult to injury! The fact is that with few honorable exceptions (like Cardinal Wyszynski of Poland and Bishop Ordass of Hungary) Iron Curtain church leaders and their official organizations are the tools of the secret police. Most of the real Christians are not in this show-case church, but in the secret Underground Church. Consider the following directives from a 1960 circular now in force, of the Committee of the Evangelistic Baptist Christians of the Soviet Union:

"The elder presbyter. . .must not care about preaching" (p. 3, par. 2)

"Less sermons and fulfilling of spiritual works... strict fulfilling of the Soviet legislation on cults" (p. 3, par. 5).

"We must strive to reduce the baptism of young ones between 18 and 30 years of age to a minimum" (p. 7, par. 3).

"Children of pre-school and school age should not as a rule be allowed to attend religious services" (p. 9, par. 6).

"In the past, not taking into consideration sufficiently the Soviet law on cults, . .there happened baptisms of men younger than 18. Charities were given from the funds of the churches. Special assemblies for Bible studies and other purposes were organized. It was permitted to recite poems. There have been excursions of believing youth. Illegal relief funds were organized. There have been meetings for instructing preachers and choir leaders. . .and there have been other violations of Soviet laws. All this must be uprooted now in our churches." (quoted from THE WURM-BRAND LETTERS. pp. 131-132)

Would ANY free Christian Church issue such directives?

Here is how real Iron Curtain Christians feel about World Council of Churches policies. The following excerpts were taken from letters to various Ecumenical leaders, written by Pastor Richard Wurmbrand, a Rumanian Lutheran pastor and former World Council of Churches representative in Rumania, who was imprisoned there, amid unspeakable tortures, for 14 years:

"I avoided writing to the World Council of Churches in Geneva for a long time, not wishing to put it under a material obligation towards me, but after I managed to secure my daily bread, I did it out of heart full of sorrow.

"This sorrow came when I read an article in the *International Review of Missions*, published by the World Council of Churches in the January, 1966 issue in which it is written, that 'the Orthodox Church and Protestantism are growing in Rumania in an atmosphere of complete religious liberty.' I asked Mr. Visser t'Hooft that if this assertion is true, then I would like to have answers to the following questions:

1. What is the address of the Bible Society in Rumania? . . .

2. Could he name one book published by a Protestant during the last 20 years?

3. What is the address of the YMCA in Rumania?

4. Could he give me the address and the hour of one Sunday school for children conducted in Bucharest?

5. What is the name and address of one charitable Christian organization in Rumania?

6. Where can I hear one Christian broadcast in Rumania?

7. Where are the pastors, Vacareanu, Nallesou, Ghelbegeanu and oth-

ers? (They are in prison for their faith.)

"There are many other similar questions which I would like to ask him.

"Why are deliberate lies told which mock the suffering of my father-land and the suffering of its church?"

Wining and Dining With Murderers

"If my barber had been put in prison for theft and would have come out, I would have gone to see him and would have helped him and asked him about his experiences in prison. I, a Rumanian pastor, after 14 years in prison, when one of the main charges against me was that I worked for the World Council of Churches, and I was asked nothing about my experiences and what I know *about* the situation in Rumania.

"The Archbishop Moisescu, about whom even the sparrows in Rumania know that he is a traitor and a man of the secret police, was banqueted in Geneva. I was in prison with 400 Christians-denounced by this same Moisescu. He reports about what happens in Rumania. To me brother Visser t'Hooft sends very kind greetings, but has never asked to speak to me. (Prof.) Hromadka, an arch-traitor who went to Moscow and was praised by Mikoyan, the right-hand man of Stalin in the mass murders of Christians, is another one who was banqueted at Geneva. But I was never given a hearing. Nobody asked me how am I living, whether I have enough to eat, (I do not need this, as I am supplied with food, but it would have been very normal to ask me this too). But what is more important, they did not ask me about what is happening in Rumania and how the Christians there are faring.

"The hearts of the Rumanian Christians are bleeding, knowing that their traitors and denunciators are embraced in Geneva and yet they are not given a chance to tell what is happening. Very politely I was told, 'Please don't come to Geneva, because the Communists will know and be irked,' just as if the Communists are dictating in Geneva too and not only in the Soviet camp.

"I asked English Church leaders, 'Why have you eaten at banquets with our inquisitors?' The answer was: 'We are Christians and must have friendship and fellowship with everybody. Including the Communists.' And I was asked if I do not agree with this Christian attitude.

"I am a man who has not read the Bible for 14 years. For 14 years I have never had a book or a piece of paper in my hands. So, surely others must know the Bible better than I do. However, I faintly remember that it is written in the Bible, 'friendship with the world is hatred towards God.' But even putting aside what the Bible says, I asked again, 'Supposing that we must have friendship and fellowship with everybody, why do you have friendship only with other inquisitors and none with their victims?'

"A high British clergyman and all the others who were with him and like him, wined and dined with our inquisitors and our betrayers. He did not leave even $100.00 for the families of Christian martyrs. The World Council of Churches and the other great bodies represented by them have never had fellowship with these. These have never experienced the love of these Christian organizations. But the Communists have. Does not the love of God extend to the bad and to the good? The love of these men however, went only to the torturers of Christians.

"I do not speak in my name. I am only a very insignificant man, and have been with the weak and little ones in prison, but I was there with heroes and saints to whom I did not dare to lift my eyes, whose shoelaces I was not worthy to tie. There were pastors in prison about whom one had the feeling that merely to touch their garment was to be made whole. Yet their children were starving at home; many of them died.

"They did not see anything of the fellowship and the friendship which the World Council of Churches and the great Christian bodies are showing to their inquisitors.

Bridges Toward Oppressors—Not Oppressed

"I speak for those who cannot speak for themselves, because they continue to be kept in chains. I am an unworthy man, but I speak for the worthiest of the Christians of the 20th century. We have had in Rumania saints and heroes like these of the first Christian centuries. Instead of their names being published everywhere in the publications of the World Council of Churches, I have always found only the names of the traitors and to them were extended words of 'understanding' and 'friendship'—to these, the murderers of Christians.

"I wonder why the Archbishop of Canterbury went to see the Pope, who is healthy and does not need his visit. He was in Rome, but why did he not go to see the graves of Catholic bishops who died in prison in Rumania? Why did he not put a flower on their graves and shed a tear there? Why did he not speak privately with one of the Protestant bishops of Rumania?"

"Pastor Milan Haimvici of Rumania has been in prison 7 years for having worked on behalf of the World Council of Churches. He has suffered great tortures to give accusatory statements against others and he did not give. He came out of Rumania. Nobody of the World Council Of Churches cared for him. A Bulgarian pastor, Popov, is now in Sweden after 13 years in Communist prisons. The World Council of Churches had not a good word or a cent for him.

"At the last Presbyterian convention, as in all the sittings of the World Council of Churches, it was decided to build bridges towards the Communist world. Towards the 1 billion people oppressed by the Communist leaders of American churches build no bridges. We did not feel your concern . . .

"Jesus teaches us to love our enemies. The murderer of my family has been converted in my house. I have brought to Christ some of my Communist jailors. I know what love towards enemies means. But how will I love an enemy if I don't love from all my heart my own country and nation? To endanger the national security of America is not a phrase. It means to endanger the lives of millions of men. . .The national security of America is a wealth of the whole free world. You endanger this in order to build bridges towards the mass murderers of Christians?"

79

Keep Mum About Hitler?

"Yesterday a Christian leader told me: 'Preach only Christ and don't preach against Communism.' I said 'Were Niemoeller, Bonhoeffer, and the others right not to preach only Christ, but to take a stand against Hitlerism?' He answered: 'Surely yes, seeing that Hitler killed 6 millions of Jews.' I said again: 'But Communists have killed 30 millions of Russians and millions of Chinese. Why is it not right to take energetically a stand against them?' His answer was: 'You are mad.'"

"When I was still in prison, the Rumanian Secret Police made me the proposal to become a Lutheran Bishop and to represent the Church in Geneva. The condition was to use Geneva for the purposes of Communism. I refused the proposal. I know what the Bishops from the East who came to Geneva are worth and who has made them Bishops. It was not the Church. It was the Secret Police. The World Council of Churches believes in speaking with the Church of the East— and speaks with the Secret Police."

"Others don't like that I am not a pacifist. Were these men pacifists when Norway was oppressed or did they like it that the American and British army came to deliver them? They are pacifists when another's fatherland is stolen. No, Pacifism is not Christian. St. Francis d'Assissi said: 'Don't shoot brother wolf, because he is also a creature of God.' If brother wolf does not give guarantee that he will not eat sister sheep, the shepherd has to shoot the wolf, if he has four legs or only two. Jesus taught us to love our enemies, but not only our enemies. We have to love our brethren, too. And if enemies attack the life and liberty of our brethren, if gangsters attack children, if Nazis burn Jews and Bolsheviks kill Christians, it is a Christian duty to fight."

What more is there to be said?

Many sincere Christians inside the World Council of Churches no doubt are not aware of these things.

But what Christian, knowing the truth, could possibly be a party to such horrors?

It is true that dedicated people have, under the auspices of the World Council of Churches and the Lutheran World Federation, done immense and precious relief and welfare work, for which thousands shall be eternally grateful. But this can, and must, be done without any ideological sell-out to Communism or secularism. Relief work justifies collaboration with the Red Revolution no more than the self-sacrifice of dedicated nuns sanctifies the Infallibility of the Pope and other enormities of the Antichrist!

At Denver (1969) the Missouri Synod will have to decide what to do not only about the A.L.C. itself, but about the whole Ecumenical spiderweb, including the World Council of Churches, of which the A.L.C. is part and parcel.

A vote for the W.C.C. is a vote against the Fourth and Fifth Commandments. It means attacking and subverting lawful govern-

80

ments, and honoring and supporting the regimes of anti-Christian and inhuman bandits and mass-murderers. It means despising the weak and toadying to the strong. It means becoming a sounding board for Communist propaganda and psychological warfare. It means helping the wolf to kill the sheep, and to do it all the more respectably. It means a cruel mocking of the suffering Church in chains, by allowing her tormentors to pose as her representatives. It means to pass by, callously, on the other side, with the Priest and the Levite. Christ did not teach us such a Sadducean "peace" and "love". He did not make common cause with Herod, the mass-murderer of Bethlehem and the assassin of John the Baptist.

Nor did His servant, Martin Luther, make common cause with the Social Gospel revolutionary, Thomas Muentzer, but condemned him in no uncertain terms. America and the world desperately need a Church which will not join in the revolutionary screeching of the enemies of God and man. We need a Church which will teach the truth in love, not lies in convenience; a Church which will speak out for the greatest Christians of modern times, the martyr-Church under Communism; a Church which will not lick the boots of revolutionaries and murderers, but call them to repentance, as St. Ambrose was not afraid to call the Emperor Theodosius himself to repentance after the terrible massacre of Thessalonica, and refused him the Sacrament until he humbled himself in Christian penitence!

The Missouri Synod can be that Church, if at Denver it seriously begins to disentangle itself from the Ecumenical nets and traps. Think of the tremendous blessings for Church and State, even to the whole world, that might result if the Missouri Synod would offer its colossal resources as a platform for warning, saving voices like Pastor Wurmbrand's—instead of lackeys and liars like Pete Seeger!

"You're from below," He told them. "I'm from above. Your home is in this world. My home is not in this world. That's why I told you, 'You will die in your sins;' if you don't believe I'm the One, you will die in your sins'"

"If God were your Father," Jesus told them, "You would love Me because I came from God, and as such I am here. . .Why don't you understand what I say? Because you can't listen to or understand what I say? Because you can't listen to what I tell you. Your father is the devil, and you want to do what your father wants. From the beginning he has been murdering people and hasn't stood in the truth, because there's no truth in him. When he tells a lie, he's telling it from his heart, because he's a liar and the father of lies. Now, because I tell the truth, you don't believe Me. Which of you can prove Me guilty of sin? If I tell the truth, why don't you believe Me? A child of-God listens to what God says. You don't listen to Him because you're not God's children."

"Aren't we right," the Jews answered Him, "When we say You're a Samaritan and there's a devil In You?"

"There's no devil in Me," Jesus answered. "No, I honor My Father, but you dishonor Me. I'm not trying to get glory for Myself. There's One who wants Me to have it, and He's the Judge. Let Me assure you: If you keep My Word, you will never see death" (St John 8:23.24.42-51, Beck's translation).

"VERILY I SAY UNTO YOU, INASMUCH AS YE HAVE DONE IT UNTO ONE OF THE LEAST OF THESE MY BRETHREN, YE HAVE DONE IT UNTO ME" (St Matthew 25:40)

Christian News, February 24, 1969

1. When commands of the civil authority cannot be obeyed without sin then ____.
2. What did LCUSA promote? ____.
3. Who effectively changed the world? ____.
4. Who was Pete Seeger? ____.
5. What was the difference between the Iron Curtain and Berlin Walls of Communism and South Africa? ____.
6. In Biafra the Christian Ibos were faced with ____.
7. The World Council of Churches dare not criticize ____.
8. Who remained forgotten? ____.
9. Jews constantly remind the world about ____.
10. Most Iron Curtain church leaders were the tools of ____.
11. Most real Christians are in ____.
12. What happened to Richard Wurmbrand? ____.
13. The Lutheran Church-Missouri Synod should have listened to Wurmbrand rather than liars like ____.
14. The greatest Christians of modern times are ____ .

REALISM: LESSONS IN CHRISTIAN DUTY - BY AN AGNOSTIC

**A Review of Frank Knopfelmacher, INTELLECTUALS
AND POLITICS (Melbourne: Nelson, 1968), 156 pp., paperback.**

If one knew nothing else about Melbourne University's Professor Knopfelnacher, one would gather from this collection of five of his essays that he is controversial. Indeed he is. He raises issues on which no one who takes social responsibility at all seriously can afford to be muddle-headed.

The temptation to quote at length is great, not only because of Knopfel-macher's gift for turning a phrase (e.g. " PR withitry" in the Church) but because of his incisive un-eggheadlike realism, which is rarely fooled by pretenses.

The first essay, "Intellectuals and Politics," makes some useful distinctions in defining the term "Intellectual," and proceeds to analyze the role of intellectuals in society. The essay takes a good look also at the intellectuals' proverbial "alienation." In describing recent trends among revolutionary intellectuals, the author comments:

"Indeed, temperamental affinities between the New Left liberated from the shackles of dogmatic Marxism, and the new Catholic Left freed from the bondage of scholastic dogmatism, may help to explain the growing co-operation between the Catholic Left and the New Left, presumably under the heading: 'Muddle-heads of the world unite! You have nothing to lose but your syllogisms' "(p. 35).

The second essay, "Catholics and Communists, a Tragi-Comedy of Errors," is of course of particular interest to Christians. Knopfelmacher argues that both the traditional anti-Communism of Rome, and the cur-rent softness towards Communism on the part of left-leaning Roman Catholics are due to a false historical analysis of Communism. The fallacy is supposed to consist in an "intellectualist" misunderstanding, which sees Marxism as a natural outgrowth of the liberal humanism and secularism of the Enlightenment, and which derives Communist practice from Communist doctrine. There may well be some truth in this charge, particularly in its second aspect. On the other hand one may well ask whether at this point Prof. Knopfelmacher's own humanistic agnosticism is not playing tricks on him. One may ask whether a deeper awareness of the reality which Christians call Original Sin may not lead to the realization that there is, after all, a connection between the inhuman brutalities of actual Communist regimes and the shiny theoretical optimism of the Enlightenment. On Christian premises at least it is certain that any attempt to build paradise without God must result in hell!

One fallacy which liberals share with traditionalists, and one might add, with observers in other churches, is the idea "that 'Marxism' represents the peaks of efficiency in welfare planning which Christians ought to 'evangelize'. At the back of this ridiculous fantasy seems to be the New

Testament story of the evil spirit who tempted Christ to change stones into loaves. In fact, of course, the rulers of communist countries do the very opposite to what the Great Tempter suggested-they invariably change loaves into stones by collectivizing agriculture and by expropriating the peasants. They are not 'materialists', but 'spiritualists' of a murky kind. The heathen paradise of purely hedonistic concerns, in which the body is amply provided for by tough-minded economic planners knowledgeable in matters of the world but indifferent to matters of the spirit, is a common bugbear in Catholic fantasies about communism, repellent to the traditionalists and attractive to the liberals. Actually the nearest approximations to such a society are the Western democracies, particularly the USA" (p. 71).

Nor is the conflict between the two tendencies fruitful:

"The effect of liberal and traditionalist Catholics on each other is mutually debilitating and deepens the confusion on both sides: the growing 'softness' of the liberal Catholic on communism tends to deepen the traditionalist disdain for all liberal attitudes, whereas the shrillness of the traditionalists anti-liberalism tends to fortify the liberal's distaste for any form of anti-communism" (p. 70).

But his most biting analytical acids Professor Knopfelmacher reserves for the left-liberal element in Australian Roman Catholicism, with special reference to the Catholic Worker group.

In a manner strikingly parallel to James Burnham's 39-point definition of the "liberal syndrome" in Suicide of the West, Knopfelmacher lists fourteen propositions as comprising "the opinion-constituents of the liberal (Roman) Catholic syndrome". (Sample: "(ix) There is a lot to be said for the Pill").

The main practical issue on which Knopfelmacher slates the left-liberal Roman Catholic intelligentsia is their flair for Christian-Communist "dialogue". Here the author makes some useful distinctions. He does not object to all transactions with Communists, but only to those in which Christians are "conned" into furthering the tactical or strategic aims of Communism. For example:

"The notion of 'dialogue' is inextricably bound up with the Church's intellectualism and with the Catholic tendency to derive communist practice from communist doctrine. Dialogue will, therefore, lead to a nebulous debate about abstract topics such as materialism, freedom, peace, etc. The communist will emerge as a splendid and dedicated humanist who is an atheist but otherwise in every way a gentleman. Needless to say, such a picture would be totally misleading. Thus, whilst not perpetuating doctrinal ' errors', 'dialogues' are likely to perpetuate empirical misconceptions about a crucial social problem" (pp. 86-87).

Another objection to 'dialogue' is that they give status and thus very important psycho-political support to the oppressors at the very time when the oppressed have begun to struggle effectively for liberation (e.g. Daniel, Sinjavsky, etc.):

"(Roman) Catholics, by allowing themselves to *be* used in the 'dialogue game' or, more crudely, by letting themselves be 'conned', are weakening

84

the very forces on whose growth the eventual liberalization of communism depends" (p. 87).

The pseudo-moral argument that "dialogue" is a duty of Christian love, regardless of the Communist participants' motives, Knopfelmacher answers with a most un-agnostic, prophetic eloquence: "appearing to do good is not the same as doing good, to participate in a public farce-staged, planned and executed by evil men for their own evil purposes-does no good at all. . .An act of 'love', undertaken in wilful ignorance of the person towards whom it is directed, ceases to be a Christian act and becomes a narcissistic gesture. In compounding an apparatchik's fraud by what appears to be an act of charity, one merely compounds fraud. The Christian who humors an apparatchik in his evil ways is acting against the apparatchik as a person in the Christian sense of the word. . .When Christ met the adulteress he forgave her, but he did not enter into a dialogue on the possible virtues of sexual license. . .When Christ met the apparatchiks of the Judah Church - State, he castigated and exposed them in parables and images of the most uncompromising ferocity. There was no dialogue with whited sepulchers" (p. 88).

Knopfelmacher sees Rome's new openness towards the Left not as a radical but as a basically conservative impulse, as part of the "unfortunate tendency of the Church to embrace expiring secular fallacies" (p. 39). (Protestant divinity students, please note as well!)

"The hidebound conservatism of the (Roman) Catholic Church which has maintained the (Roman) Catholic intellectual ghetto extends into the policy of the aggiornamento, since what the Church is now willing to recognize, 'optimistic liberalism' and ' Marxism' , are creeds already well on the way to the rubbish-heap of history. As long as there was fire and faith in liberalism and hope in the policies of the Marxists, the Church acted as the spiritual policeman of the European reactionaries and maintained a rigid posture of unyielding condemnation. . .What was denied to the living Faith is now freely given to the dying creed: the blessings of the Holy Mother Church. Pope Paul's pointless trip to the UN, interpreted rather comically as a 'livid' and 'modern' gesture, can now be seen for what it has turned out to be—a religious ceremony at the burial in the vaults of the Vatican of 'official liberalism' with full ecclesiastic honors" (p. 89)

Finally, Knopfelmacher evaluates the mentality represented by the Catholic Worker, which he finds 'holy', unctuously pious, bitchy in a personal sort of way, contra-social, and politically 'innocent'. It is the writing of prey who haven't seriously thought about Marxism as social theory but who have picked up cliche's about it along with cliché's about other areas of 'the contemporary'" (p. 99). And: "The paper's religious style has all the passion of the Proceedings of the Royal Optical Society and the spiritual depth of sermons to the Methodist Ladies' College" (p. 97).

Within this mentality Knopfelmacher distinguishes two strains, the church-oriented and the University oriented. The latter's favored style of discourse is said to be "the Wittgensteinian esoteric goulash—lots of unfinished sentences, grunts, platitudes dished out with an air of philosophical depth, and a great show of boyish "sincerity" (p. 105).

After stating and examining a number of theories about "Catholic Worker group behavior" Knopfelmacher illustrates his own. In essence it is this, that the Catholic Worker and the mentality it represents do not really care about religious or political principles as such, but manipulates them as just symbols or badges of ideological respectability. "The deference objects define their reference group: the left-liberal, largely Protestant, intelligentsia and their activities, institutions, postures, rituals and prevailing political attitudes."

In order to gain acceptance within the academic establishment, the socially "upward mobile" Roman Catholic intelligentsia apes the "in" values, whilst bitterly repudiating elements perceived as threatening these status-aspirations, e.g. the anti-communism of Santamaria and the N.C.C. Should this mentality prevail, says Knopfelmacher,

"The formidable figure of the Australian 'Mick,' the Communist Party's most implacable and skilled opponent, would disappear from the Australian landscape, to be replaced by a collection of gentlemen of doubtful authenticity and in borrowed, ill-fitting clothes, for whom politics and religion are coded items in a status game played for their own personal stakes" (p. 115).

Thus the paper is simply "the product of a groping, socio-cultural cringe to an amorphous reference group."

Moreover, the "gentlemen of doubtful authenticity" have, with their "sociocultural cringe," succeeded in breaking down the academic Left's implacable hostility to Roman Catholicism. This however is due not to any supposed missionary value of the "cringe," but to the realization on the part of the Left "that (Roman) Catholicism as such, unless accompanied by specific interpretations and specific organizational forms, can be as harmless as Anglican, and (Roman) Catholic liberals as useful as the Dean of Canterbury"(p. 110)!

I have treated this matter in such detail not because of any deep interest in the Catholic Worker as such, but because of the obvious parallels to the problems of the intelligentsia in other confessional churches, the Lutheran in particular. Substitute "German confessionals" for "Irish traditionalism" and you can document the same defensive over-compensations, the same status anxieties, the same "socio-cultural cringe" to current academic fads and fashions. By taking Knopfelmacher's dissection of the Catholic Worker as paradigmatic, Lutheran university students can at least become aware of some of the more obvious pitfalls inherent in their own situation.

In conclusion, let us sample the third essay, "On Tolerance".

Countering much rhetorical sloganeering with words like "tolerance" and "prejudice," the writer shows that it "often happens that a group with an ideology consisting almost entirely of prejudice is very tolerant, in that it does not press strife pursued in the name of its false notions too far. On the other hand, groups whose ideas are closely matched by fact may be absolutely ruthless." Analytical clarity is valuable, but it cannot excuse from the obligation to make moral decisions:

"It has become fashionable among some people to extend the meaning of the term 'prejudice' in an unwarranted manner, so as to cover any strongly held belief or value, irrespective of truth or falsity. The habit of philosophical doubt, which is a perfectly legitimate device of analytical philosophy, has been stretched to justify lack of commitment in fundamental matters of social policy, and it has been misused to encourage an attitude of mock - serene connivance towards totalitarian conspiracies directed against pluralism. While it must be freely conceded at once that *both* the spokesmen of the enslaved and those who speak on behalf of their masters are using language in a systematically misleading manner, it seems important that they are using it for different purposes. The spokesmen of the victims advocate the exaltation of concentration-camp regimes, while the spokesmen of the masters are trying to justify them. This difference of purpose, and not the relative logical purity of discourse, prompts us to take sides" (p. 123).

This issue of morality vs. formalistic pedantry becomes pretty concrete:

"Men who are conspiring to inflict unspeakable misery on the Australian worker and on everybody else—the communists—are accepted as bona fide trade union leaders and are given extensive opportunities to corrupt working-class organizations by turning them into instruments of foreign slave-owners. Our 'liberal' intellectuals meanwhile confess that they are incapable of choosing between the rival fanaticisms of those who wish to escape the concentration camps and those who are plotting to erect them. They find the rule of the indoctrinated gorilla indistinguishable from passionate opposition to it" (pp. 128-129).

Knopfermacher argues that a tolerant, pluralistic society can survive only if it defends its institutional basis against external and internal assault. But the mentality of "shallow cynicism and intellectual mushiness" aptly described as "social scientism" by Knopfelmacher cannot motivate this necessary defense. On the contrary, it "breeds a kind of tolerance which stems from indifference and is , therefore, self-destructive, since it undermines the political foundations of freedom" (p. 127).

Intellectuals addicted to "social scientism" often exhibit a selective credulity about Communism "which must be regarded as pathological, coming as it does from professional intellectuals with impressive records of skill in critical analysis. Simple error of fact and lack of information cannot explain a monumental lapse of sound judgment about an important subject on which information is now fully available. Without examining the causes of the pathology. . .two things of practical consequence must be borne in mind. First, people who are or at least were prepared to believe that power-technicians addicted to genocide can set the stage for a secular paradise are a group with a very wide margin of irrationality and, therefore, highly manipulable. The second consequence relates to debunking which is alleged to be the proper pursuit of the enlightened educator, writer, and journalist. If those who debunk entertain at the same time little private delusions about a Kingdom of Heaven being under construction just round the corner in Chicago slave-cities and in similar places, they will be thoroughly one-sided and selective. None of

87

our own accepted beliefs and values will escape hostile and damaging scrutiny. The failings of the Open Society will be ruthlessly exposed in a most penetrating manner. Yet somehow, along the way, communist bunk will be spared and treated with gentle reticence or halting equivocation. Unilateral debunking of this kind creates a completely distorted picture of the world, and it paves the way for unilateral disarmament, moral neutralism and surrender" (p. 126).

Behind this amoral and irrational social scientist there lurks psychoanalytic ideology, which has been reigning, with disastrous effects "ever since Freud replaced Calvin as the accredited prophet of the Anglo-American bourgeoisie" (p. 125)!

As a result of the Vietnam debate, Knopfelmacher is prepared to concede more to the "illuminating in-sights of depth-psychology" than when he wrote " On Tolerance"; for, as he says in the Preface, the Vietnam excitement has convinced him "that the public stage of political and ideological polemics in our seemingly sheltered consumer society is a facade for transactions which are unconscious or semi-conscious and which are almost completely unconnected with the substance of the debated issues."

Yet some of the earlier strictures seem still valid:

"The current American philosophy of education which values social skills, group harmony, and 'integration' above everything else in life stems directly from psychoanalytic ideology. The frantic desire to be 'loved' at all costs, and the belief that ideas and arguments do not really matter if you can manipulate biological and conditioned drives and incentives appropriately, are some consequences, with the more obviously disastrous political corollaries" (p. 125).

Christian readers of the Knopfelmacher essays will realize that it is not enough to chatter about "involvement". Political irresponsibility which results in misery for millions is sin, and is not excused by invoking the pretext of Christian liberty. "The legitimacy of silliness ends this side of the mass graves" (. 92)! That is mere natural justice. Does not Christian love for the neighbor involve even more?

Christian News, September 28, 1970

1. Any attempt to build a paradise without God must result in ____.
2. When does an act of love cease to be a Christian act? ____
3. When Christ met the adulteress he ____.
4. There was no dialogue with ____.
5. Simple error of fact and lack of information cannot explain ____.
6. Political irresponsibility which results in misery for millions is ____.

STOP COMMUNIST AGGRESSION

The Honorable Thomas P. O'Neill, Jr.
U. S. House of Representatives
WASHINGTON, D.C.
U.S.A.

Sir:
As an American living in the South East Asian region I am ashamed and horrified to read in the press that there is likely to be much opposition in Congress to President Ford's request for increased aid to South Vietnam in its desperate fight for survival.

No informed person can doubt that:

(1) Vietnam is not a "Civil War" but one of naked aggression by the Hanoi Stalinists against South Vietnam, Laos, and Cambodia.

(2) Without adequate U.S. aid (in terms of the Paris Accord) South Vietnam must fall to the aggressors, who are being armed by Soviet and Maoist powers.

(3) Any further expansion of Soviet and/or Maoist power bases is contrary to the legitimate self-interest of the U.S.A. and of the free World.

(4) The deliberate surrender of millions to certain slavery and slaughter flies in the face of America's humanitarian professions. (One former Viet Cong province chief said that three million South Vietnamese alone are marked for liquidation!)

I add only that after Solzhenitsyn any further illusions about Soviet realities are obscene. Hence any repetitions today of the horrors of Yalta must be branded as wilful and cold-blooded crimes against humanity. And a society which is prepared to buy ease and comfort for itself by periodically sacrificing smaller countries to Stalinist molochs, cannot and does not deserve to survive. It has become a loathsome vampire.

If these realities will simply be swept under the carpet of petty party-politics, the result will predictably be disastrous—and America and her Congress will incur the just condemnation and contempt of humanity and of history!

Can you therefore give the clear and unequivocal assurance, in the name of plain human decency, that you will do your utmost, as a leader in Congress, to prevent the longsuffering victims of communist aggression in Vietnam from being thrown to the Wolves?

Yours faithfully,
K. Marquart
Christian News, April 7, 1975

1. Vietnam was not a "civil war" but ____.
2. After Solzhenitsyn any illusions about Soviet realities are ____ .

THE FORGOTTEN PEOPLE

"Remember My Chains!"(Colossians 4:18)

When our dear Lord, in the institution of His Holy Supper, was planting the Tree of Life in the very center of His New Testament Temple, the Church, He said: "Do this IN REMEMBRANCE of Me!"

But He does not allow us to "remember" Him while forgetting His people! We cannot honor the Head, if we neglect and despise His members, especially His suffering members. "I was in prison and you came to visit Me," Christ will say to us on Judgment Day, for "whatever you did for one of the least of these brothers of Mine, you did for Me" (St. Matthew 25:36-40). And a stunned persecutor of "mere people" is confronted by the God-Man Himself, demanding: "Saul, Saul, why do you persecute ME?" (Acts 9:4).

Fashionable Crusading

The suffering millions, especially the Christians, in the communist slave empire are undoubtedly the world's Most Forgotten People. Every little disadvantaged minority in our world receives the tender attentions of the keepers of our public conscience. It is quite fashionable to crusade even for the well-being of wild animals, trees, lakes, and inanimate things like burial grounds.

But by current media manners it is OBSCENE to mention the killed and tormented millions in the Red hell! In our country people are sent to goal for lesser cruelties to cats and dogs than are daily and routinely committed against our fellow Christians In Russia, China, and the other slave states!

The classic description of our upside-down, half sentimental, half cruel "public opinion", comes from the eloquent pen of Alexander Solzhenitsyn:

"When the racial composition of a basketball team proves to be a bigger world event than the daily injections given to the captives in our psychiatric prisons to destroy their brains, then what else can you feel but contempt for an egotistic, shortsighted and defenseless civilization?" (Moscow interview, 23 August, 1973).

Do We Care?

V. Chernyshov, a mathematician imprisoned in a Leningrad psychiatric prison, wrote:

"Christians! Your brothers in Christ are Suffering. Stand up for their souls! Christians! Do not allow them to give a healthy man drugs that will destroy his soul. . . . I am afraid of death, but I'll accept it. I'm terribly afraid of torture. But there is a worse torture, and it awaits me — the introduction of chemicals into my mind. The vivisections of the 20th century will not hesitate to seize my soul; maybe I will remain alive, but after this I won't be able to write even one poem; I won't be able to think, I have already been informed of the decision for my 'treatment'.

Farewell!" (Bukovsky Papers).

The Soviet publication *Doshkolnoye Vospitanie* (Preschool Education) of March, 1966, shows a picture of four praying children being seized by the police for "re-education" away from the "poison" of the Bible!

Who Is That Woman?

Komsomolskaya Pravda (Communist Youth League Truth) of May 22, 1966, told of 9-year old Kolya Sviridov, who was taken away from his Christian family and placed in an atheistic boarding school. Since he continued to pray, he was handed over to the personal custody of Captain Hutorin of State Security, who made him repeat: "There are no gods!" When his mother was allowed to see him, the boy asked: "Who is that woman?"

And when reports about these hellish inhumanities leak out to the West, or appeals are sent, what happens to them?

In his excellent Monday Club (London) tract, *The Crooked Conscience,* Bernard Smith refers to Georgi Vins, a Russian Baptist, arrested in 1966 for his Christian faith and life:

"Details of Vins's trial and of others were given in a letter sent by relatives of imprisoned Baptists to U Thant, former Secretary-General of the United Nations. That was in August, 1967. In December, when no reply had been received, one of the signatories, Mrs. Yakimenkova, mother of seven children, risked her freedom by going to Moscow and seeking out Western correspondents. She was reported in the London papers as saying: 'Surely someone is listening to our appeals? Surely someone will help us? Can't you tell U Thant that we have heard nothing from him?'

"Nothing ever was heard from U Thant. Nor was anything heard from the United Nations Commission on Human Rights to whom the appeal was also sent. Nor from the International Commission of Jurists. Nor from the Baptist World Alliance. Nor from the World Council of Churches. They all had copies of the appeal but none of them ever replied. 'Surely someone is listening to our appeals' said Mrs. Yakimenkova. To which the short answer is - No. No one is listening. No one."

Can Something Be Done?

God IS listening! He hears the innocent blood crying to Heaven! He also sees and hears whether we are prepared to help, of whether we shut our eyes, ears, and hearts, and sink back into the "fun and games" stupor of our rotten society!

Nicolai Khamara became a Christian at age 47, and was sent to prison for "religious activities".

A fortnight later his wife received back his dead body, full of bruises and marks of torture. AND HIS TONGUE HAD BEEN CUT OUT!

We who have tongues, and the freedom to use them, must speak and cry out for those who cannot! As Bonhoeffer said about Nazi persecution: "Whatever does not scream out on behalf of the Jews, has no right to chant his litanies either!"

91

[Further information can be obtained from "The Christian Mission to the Communist World" Box 34, Miranda, N.S.W., which publishes a free monthly bulletin. (U. S. Address: Box 11, Glendale, California, ed.)

Get this sort of information and spread it around. Next to personal prayers and actual gifts this publicity is of the greatest possible help to our suffering fellow Christians!

Encounter for Lutheran Youth, Australia, December 1974
Christian News, January 27, 1975

1. Who were the world's most forgotten people? ____.
2. What is worse than temporal death? ____.

HANDING HELPLESS RUSSIANS
TO THE COMMUNISTS

Churchmen claim that it is the Church's responsibility to protest against injustices throughout the world. CN has often noted the double standard of many liberal churchmen who are constantly complaining about the lack of human rights in South Africa, Chile, South Korea, or some other "right-wing" nation but who have little to say about the ruthless mass murders performed by the Communists in Afghanistan and elsewhere.

Years ago, as a teenager preparing for the ministry in a Lutheran Church-Missouri Synod prep school shortly after World War II, we spoke in class about what we at that time referred to as "one of the great crimes of the ages," U.S. participation in the forcing of helpless Russians and Eastern Europeans back to the Communists. We said that some churchmen, who thought they were such great "scholars," seemed to be rather ignorant about Communism and what was going on in the world. A few of our professors thought that there must be something wrong with us when we complained about Yalta and President Franklin Roosevelt's part in this forced repatriation.

When one of them asked where we got our information, we mentioned that one of our sources was a book titled "CRIME OF THE AGES" and that, Dr. Walter A. Maier, at that time the Lutheran Hour speaker, said that the book told the truth. Our LCMS professor, who had a master's degree in history, said Maier didn't know what he was talking about and was no scholar when it came to history and world affairs. Maier only had a Ph.D. in the Old Testament from Harvard.

Professor Kurt Marquart

While at Concordia Seminary, St. Louis, we roomed with an Estonian who had to leave Estonia after the Communists takeover had begun. His mother and step-father had been born in Russia. More than 10 years later the October 7, 1968 *Christian News* published a speech this refugee from Communism, Professor Kurt Marquart, now teaching at the LCMS's seminary in Fort Wayne, Indiana, gave on May 11, 1968 at the Second Annual Seminar of the Australian League of Rights held in Brisbane, Australia. The entire speech is in our *Christian Handbook on Vital Issues*. Professor Marquart began this great speech, which should be printed in the LCMS's *Lutheran Witness*:

[Editor's note: This section of "Handing Helpless Russians to the Communists" is on pages 62-64]

Operation Keelhaul

When the Devin-Adair Company, One Park Ave. , Old Greenwich, Corm., published Julius Epstein's Operation Keelhaul, the January 14, 1974 *Christian News* featured the book in its lead story. Epstein told about the forced repatriation of more than one million Soviet nationals

93

back to Stalin's firing squads and slave labor camps in 1945 and later, after the end of World War II. Most church publications ignored this important book. (See The *Christian News Encyclopedia*, p. 497.)

Last week we received the following letter and article from Dr. Clarence Lang, an ALC professor who knows what is going on in the world.

January 19, 1987
Christian News
Pastor Herman Otten, Editor

Dear Editor:
Some years ago while researching in the Ecumenical Library in Geneva, Switzerland; I found mimeographed-typed descriptions of strange happenings in Kempten, Germany in1945. This was in one of the personal files. I spotted this again in my files and thought it should be shared with readers of the CN. Obviously, for the writer English was a foreign language. Everything in (—) was added for clarity.

Readers may regard this as a sequel to my translation of Dr. Walter Bodenstein's IST NUR DER BESIEGTE SCHULDIG? (IS ONLY THE LOSER GUILTY?). This incident occurred two months before eleven German churchmen confessed the Stuttgart Confession of German Guilt, and about three months after the capitulation of Germany — even after our victory over Japan. If you print this in the CN, it will memorialize those helpless Russians who were handed over to Stalin by the Americans. (Kempten is hundreds of miles from the then Russian Zone).Isn't it understandable that those Germans who heard about such happenings, as well as, those unfortunately Americans who were forced to carry out such orders would be confused at the unilateral demand on the part of Allied churchmen for German repentance? Some had justifiable reasons to disagree when they heard men as the Swiss Karl Barth pontificate that the American planes and Russian tanks were God's instruments to teach the Germans and the world a lesson.

Sincerely,
R. Clarence Lang, Ph.D.
814 East College
Seguin, Texas 78155

RUSSIAN displaced Persons Camp Wittelsbacher School
KEMPTEN
Kempten, August 15th, 1945
On the 12th August 1945 in the Russian camp in Kempten (acuity S.W. from Munich) events have taken place which not only had a tragically end to many of the inhabitants of the camp, but considering the violation of the elementary humanitarian principles they draw the attention of all those, who presume that the time of rehabilitation of freedom and respect to the human rights has come.

On (the) 12 August 1945, Sunday morning, the usual Sunday life of the camp began, and though on Saturday some rumors were heard of a possibility of forced dispatch to U.S.S.R. of the so called new emigrants, in as much as there was no official announcement on this matter, this was considered to be one of the rumors disquieting the camp inhabitants which never occurred before. Notwithstanding the anxiety most of the camp inhabitants as always went at the usual time to the religious service to the camp church.

At 10:15 a.m. trucks drove to the gate of the camp, and soon arrived a detachment of the American soldiers. This news became in a moment known in the camp and having presentiment of a coming of some decisive moment all hastened to the church as if seeking there (their) last protection by the One, Who 19 centuries ago has called to Himself all the sufferings. Here, in the church, the old and the new emigration have particularly sharply felt their defenselessness for the human laws, their unity, their brotherhood of blood and spirit. And so it really was, because the new emigration has left their country on the same cause, as the old one. Naturally, the old emigration could have one normal feeling-not to forsake their next of kin in peril.

No sooner was the service ended, the chief of the camp, general Daniloff, appeared on the choir and announced that the American trucks have arrived in order to dispatch to U.S.S.R. all those who were before 1938 within its boundaries. This announcement has caused a deep sorrow among the congregation. There were cries: "We do not want to go there, we would rather die here." Then the commandant read the list of names-410 persons-who were immediately to be put in American trucks.

Among the persons whose names were called, a panic broke out. But at this time an American officer entered the church and in presence of general Daniloff, who came down from the choir, announced through an interpreter that those who must be dispatched should go to one side of the church, and then on- dispatched to the other, the order was repeated 3 times. People losing their senses with grief did not move; many precipitated to the American officer imploring him for mercy. Weeping mothers reached him (officer) their children, old people and young women stood on their knees before him kissed his hands and entreating him not to send them to U.S.S.R.; the picture of sorrow was so genuinely (sic) real that even those who were not to be turned over were crying, because they understood these people's grief and understanding for the humanity. The officer has brought soldiers and about 7 of them entered the church their rifles ready in their hands. There were heard (sic) cries among the women, some of them fainted and had to be restored to their senses. The officer left the church with the soldiers but returned in 15-20 minutes with a new detachment. The expulsion of the Russians from the church began. The people took each other by hand deciding not to leave the church of their own will, because they knew well (wording unclear) expected them outside. The soldiers seized men and women by hands, beat them with the fists, with the handles of the revolvers, stoke (sic) them with the butts of their rifles disunited people holding each other, tore

95

clothes on them, pulled men and women by their hair, tearing the hair from their heads, dragged them on the floor through whole church and threw them into the corridor where other soldiers with blows and rifles-butts hurled them farther. There Russians were near insanity with despair. But not a single of them had even touched an American soldier. They did not touch them even then, when one of the soldiers seized the old priest by the beard and dragged him through the church and when another soldier struck the other old clergyman, holding the Cross in his hands, with the fist in the face, trying to pull the Cross out of his hands. Many women were severely beaten up, or scratched over the body; an old man had his ribs broken. Women had histerics (sic) and fainted, the yells of the massacred were heard far outside the church, and even outside of the camp. Several shots were fired in the church. Some of the people, even with the children jumped out of the windows into the narrow passage of the court-yard, trying to save them in flight. The soldiers shot at them. Two people were severely wounded, one of them into the stomach. Twelve other people were carried on to hospitals, in their number those with broken ribs.

The church was evacuated. The church room represented a chaotic picture. The Altar in the apse was overturned the holy images were thrown on the floor, the candle sticks were broken, the holy images on the altar-screen damaged, the altar screen itself severely damaged, especially the left side, the balus-trade before the apse destroyed, flowers and green leaves decorating the church were trumped on the floor, on the floor were scattered morsels of broken vases, pieces of torn clothes, handkerchiefs, shoes, etc.

The shocked people were led into the yards of the camp the injured were carried on hand barrows, also the fainted. Here the documents were examined, and (the) to be-dispatched people were immediately put in trucks not leaving them even the time to go upstairs and collect their belongings. Only several of them received such permission. But the majority of them left without having the possibilities to pick up the most necessary things. Some hand-barrows with motionless bodies were also loaded in the trucks.

Christian News, February 2, 1987

1. What did Kurt Marquart witness about helpless Russians? ____.
2. The Red Counter Revolution replaced not the Czar but ____.
3. What were some of the horrors performed by the Che-ka? ____.
(p. 63)
4. What is Operation Keelhaul? ____.
5. What happened to helpless Russians handed over to Stalin by the Americans? ____.

TWO DOCUMENTS ON
CHURCH AND STATE

Introductory Note: Having been asked for something on Church-State relations, I submit two items which may be of interest. The first is a statement by the Queensland District (Australia) Pastors' Conference (May, 1972) concerning the Action for World Development campaign sponsored jointly by the Australian Council of Churches and the Roman Catholic Church of Australia.

The second document is a memorandum I submitted to the Australia-wide Conference on Racism which met near Brisbane in November, 1971, under the auspices of the Australian Council of Churches and the Roman Catholic Church. The conference was intended for churchmen connected with Christian education. I attended as one of the two official observers for the Lutheran Church of Australia, which is not a member of the Australian Council of Churches.

The two statements indicate, I think, in terms of concrete particulars, why any attempt to set up a "Christian" political party or program must inevitably collapse: if it is at all concrete and specific, as a genuine political party or program must be, it will necessarily involve judgments on which even doctrinally agreed Christians will differ.

It would seem that unlike Roman and Calvinistic concepts of theocracy, Luther's Two-Kingdom doctrine is not only theologically correct, but is actually the only workable option in our pluralistic societies.

One final comment: Luther's insistence that the State must be governed not by revelation but by reason and that reason is sufficient for this, must not be misunderstood. For Luther "reason" was not the modern positivistic notion of abstract rationality, cut off from all absolutes and "values," but the intellect as it is rooted in conscience and the (natural) Moral Law. Without such a starting point in absolute moral standards, reason cannot of itself produce compelling moral norms, without which in turn social organization is impossible—except in the form of arbitrary tyranny a la Stalin. Evolutionary naturalism or scientism cannot possibly generate moral obligations. If there is no God and man is but a freak of nature, then his life is no more sacred that than of rats, mosquitoes, or germs! And from purely descriptive scientific statements about what is, no ethical principles about what ought to be, can possibly be deduced by any conceivable logical process.

In the sense that basically amoral, atheistic assumptions are more and more openly shaping practical political programs (e.g. abortion on demand), the religious issue is bound to arise much more urgently than in previous ages, when all parties shared a more or less common platform of Christian assumptions. But this still does not imply a directly "Christian" politics. The proper Christian contribution to politics happens more indirectly, in terms of natural law, accessible to conscience, reason, and common sense. The appeal is to the citizen's moral sense, to what is just and fair, rather than to anything specifically Christian. And while re-

97

vealed, Biblical Christianity is the only true, adequate, and consistent foundation for the socially necessary concept of morally-grounded reason, this concept is also held by, say, Jews, Mormons, and theists generally, all of whom will therefore tend to form a common front, on the civic level, against atheists and moral nihilists of all kinds. In this sense "Christian" politics is not distinctively Christian at all.

A. Statement of Pastors' Conference re.
Action for World Development Campaign

1. Christians have the clear obligation of love to use the political power of citizenship in the service of their neighbor's welfare.

2. The exercise of responsible citizenship, however, involves information, competence, and judgments on which the Church as Church (Matt. 28:19ff) is neither qualified nor authorized to make pronouncements, and which must therefore be left to each individual Christian citizen, acting according to such insights as he has, and in association with political parties and groups of his own choice.

3. Because this vital distinction between the Church's proper task and the Christian's own civic responsibilities is ignored, even erased, in the materials published by the current Action for Worlds Development campaign, we cannot recommend these materials as an adequate basis for an approach to Christian civic action.

4. We further note that the materials are open to the charge of ideological one-sidedness, e.g. "injustice" and "inequality" are presented exclusively in contexts suggesting Western "capitalism" as the real villain, without any mention of Communism.

5. However, we encourage our people to take an active interest in the needs of developing nations as a practical expression of their Christian love.

B. Memorandum to Racism Conference:
"A Plea for Christian Balance on the Race Issue"

Is there a distinctively Christian view?
That a conference of Christian educators should deal with the ugliness and injustice of racism is surely a most welcome development.

There are of course other groups in the community concerned with race related problems. Of a Christian conference one would expect a specifically Christian contribution. Unless a conscious effort is made to think about race in terms of Christian teaching and perspective, we are in danger of simply taking over a piece of ready-made secular-liberal ideology. Christian verbiage may still be used with it, but it functions merely as a fig-leaf for a secular position, which has long ago made its unilateral declaration of independence from the authority of God and His revelation.

Much of our discussion so far (this is being written after Saturday's sessions) seems to me to have been somewhat nebulous, partly because of a failure to define basic Christian premises and to make some necessary distinctions.

What is the function of the Church?

For instance, no clear distinction has been made between Church and society, and their entirely different natures, standard, and functions. As we fervently accuse ourselves of racism, it seems to make no real difference whether "we" means "we Christians, members of Christ's Body," or "we as members of white Australian society". Surely the two are not synonymous!

If the Church is understood in a secular-reformist sense, as a "sector" of society in general, the distinction between the two is of course unimportant. But if the Church is seen in the radical New Testament sense, as God's baptized people, meeting regularly with their Resurrected King, who distributes life, strength, and salvation through His Gospel and the mystery of His sacramental Presence, then the Church's task differs totally from that of secular society.

Christians, to be sure, have civic obligations and ought to be active in the civic sphere. But the Church as Church has only one clear, divine directive, one set of marching orders (Matt. 28:18ff), and that has nothing whatever to do with politics or civic structures as such.

Clear Principles

This implies, for me at least, that the churches and their educational agencies have a right to expect from this Conference, clear formulations about how Christian commitment effects one's relations with people of other races. It would be pointed out, for instance, that race must be seen in the context of the actual unity of mankind in terms of creation, of sin, judgment, death, etc., and of its potential new unity in Christ, the life-giving Word of God to and for all men, and the Head and Foundation of the new humanity (Rom. 5). This means that within the fellowship of this new humanity racial and other differences simply do not matter any longer (Gal. 3:28)—although these distinctions do not thereby automatically lose their significance in the general social structure. But whatever may happen "outside", the gathering that is conscious of being the Lord's Body, meeting in His Name around His Meal cannot possibly tolerate divisions based on race or similar trivia.

If Australian parishes are in many cases failing to reflect the interracial Christian reality, perhaps the real cause is not at all racial, but religious and theological. Do parishes take themselves seriously enough as the Family of God in that place, gathered in Him and for His work? Is apathy toward the Aborigine simply part and parcel of a general indifference toward the un-churched masses—and toward Christ's Great Commission? I am merely asking, not accusing.

Relevant Christian instruction must go further. It must impress on Christ's people the seriousness of their civic obligations, both in terms of respect for lawful authority in society (Rom. 13)—this dare not be sentimentalized away for the benefit of anarchists and revolutionaries—and of that social justice which I owe my neighbor as part of my love for him, and in direct proportion to my own political right, power and influence. But precisely how I must put this love into practice in all sorts of concrete

99

and complex situations, is something the corporate Church has neither the right nor the duty to tell me. Christian citizens, acting individually or collectively in situations whose normal dimensions are not clearly defined in revelation, must accept responsibility for their own decisions. And it often happens in this realm of civic action that the judgment of equally serous Christians differs radically. This has to be accepted in love, without any attempt to tyrannize anyone else's conscience.

A "Christian" Immigration Policy?

On these grounds I question the right of any Christian spokesman to state or imply that a particular political program is "the Christian" approach, say, to New Guinea's independence or to Australian immigration policy—examples repeatedly cited in this Conference!

It is perfectly possible for thoughtful Christians to be opposed to early independence for New Guinea. One may argue that premature independence will lead to bitter tribal conflict and will precipitate the sort of tragic bloodbaths and genocide which have occurred in hastily "liberated" states in Africa. Informed Christian concern will then concentrate on adequate and proper preparation for self-government, rather than on formal independence as an end in itself.

Or take immigration. A Christian may welcome members of all races into his neighborhood, street, or home. Yet experience and observation may have convinced him that no satisfactory model of a well-functioning inter-racial or multi-racial society exists, and that Australian society as a whole would suffer from the disruption of its present relative cultural homogeneity which would follow large-scale immigration from, say, Africa or Asia. I do not say that this view which it is perfectly possible for a Christian to hold, without being guilty of "racism", i.e. malice toward any human being because of his race.

The unfortunate tendency of "Ecumenical" bodies to pontificate on this sort of issue is effectively analyzed in Paul Ramsey, Who Speaks for the Church (Edinburgh: St. Andrew Press, 1969).

Christian Truth vs. Relativism, Revolution, Ideology

There are important questions of principle, raised at this conference, which can and ought to be clearly resolved on strictly Christian grounds.

In the first place, there have been suggestions of what I can only describe as religious relativism, e.g. that Indians could be Christians without having heard of Christ, or that it is "racist" to assert the superiority of Christianity over the religious beliefs of pre-Christian Australian Aborigines. These notions were not taken up for discussion. Perhaps they were not taken seriously. But they are too fundamental to be ignored.

It is true enough that Christianity has often become entangled with political, social, and cultural interests of all sorts, which non-European Christians may rightly reject. But the fact remains that Christianity makes exclusive and absolute claims, and necessarily rejects other religions as false. And Christianity's truth-claims must be examined and decided on grounds that have nothing whatever to do with race. Once I

100

have accepted the Resurrected Asian, Jesus Christ, as God Incarnate, I am committed to the exclusive worship of the Most Holy Trinity as the only true God. I cannot then make relativistic concessions to other religions. (In this connection I'd like to recommend two recent books, **Christianity: The Witness of History** and **Comparative Religion,** both by J.N.D. Anderson, O.B.E., LL.D., Professor of Oriental Laws and Director of the Institute of Advanced Legal Studies in the University of London).

To demand such concessions is to demand that the Church denature herself, and give up the one thing which it is her sacred duty to share with Indian and Eskimo, Jew and Aborigine. But by sharing the uncompromised fullness of God's mercy in Christ with the Aborigine, the Church gives him something infinitely greater that land-rights, reduced infant-mortality, or plumbing: she gives him life, truth, meaning, in short, his true place in God's scheme of things. If this is "paternalistic," then so is the New Testament. And if Christian churches cannot act confidently and unambiguously on the basis of their own original charter and constitution, what right or reason have they to continue to exist? "Social concern", is no substitute for spiritual substance and cannot fill the void that faces the detribalized Aborigine, dispossessed of his old religion, yet unclaimed by another. That void will then be filled by demons like secularism, Marxism, anarchy, alcohol, etc.

Secondly, I emphatically protest against any interpretation of Christ as a political revolutionary. His enemies, the Pharisees, had such ideas, and even His disciples had to be disabused of political expectations. But He Himself clearly taught that His Kingdom is not of this world. He preached not revolution or "national liberation," but giving to Caesar what was Caesar's. He came to liberate men from the bonds of sin and death, not those of political oppression.

I deeply deplore the prominence of anarchist-revolutionary thinking in leading World Council of Churches circles, and I cannot approve the W.C.C.'s monetary and "moral" support of Communist-influenced terrorists in Southern Africa!

A far better example of real Christianity is the heroic martyrs suffering and dying in Communist prisons and torture- chambers. They do not hate and curse their tormentors, but love and forgive them—thereby winning converts even from among the secret police itself! Innocent suffering for Christ's sake is something beautiful and precious, full of the divine dignity of Him Who forgave His murderers, and Whose mind is to form ours (Phil. 2:5 ff. I Pet. 2:13-25).

(On the plight of Christians under Communism see Michael Bourdeaux, Religious Ferment in Russia, Robert Conquest, Religion in the USSR, and, for a personal account, Richard Wurmbrand, Christian the Communist Prisons).

Where Christian Aborigines suffer injustice, they cannot react more nobly than with love and forgiveness—and it is the Church's duty to teach this element of basic Christianity. Nor does this preclude peaceful, lawful attempts at redress. But ultimate love and forgiveness are more powerful than hate and revenge. At least that is what Christians believe on good authority.

(See also Thomas Molnar's Utopia, **The Perennial Heresy** (New York: Sheed and Ward, 1967) for an analysis of the unrealistic, anti-Christian assumptions of modern revolutionary movements, which begin by trying to build on earth a paradise without God, and end by creating the closest approximations to hell—such as Mao Tse-Tung's communes!)

Thirdly, I object to a treatment of Holy Scripture which can drag it (Ezra 9!) before the judgment seat of a pre-conceived notion of "racism," and pronounce it guilty! Christians are accustomed to the reverse procedure: human philosophies and ideologies are judged in the light of revealed, divine truth, not vice versa!

Racism or Reality?

Finally—and this is a question not of theology but of plain factual accuracy—I question both the truthfulness and the usefulness of the sweeping, all-embracing notions of "race" and "racism" that have frequently been expressed at this Conference. Race is one among many facts of human life, but it is not the key to reality that some seem to imagine it to be.

For example, much of what has been cited at this Conference as "racism," need not be interpreted as anything of the kind. It could be taken simply as an instance of a much more general apathy. I know from personal experience how difficult it is to stir up sustained public concern about the fate of any group of people, be they white or of whatever color! How many people really care about the oppression of China by Mao's gang, who are reliably estimated to have murdered some 50 million people? (*The Human Cost of Communism in China*, by China expert Prof. Richard Walker, Director of the Institute of International Studies in the University of South Carolina). Who really cares whether the West abandons South Vietnam to Communist aggression and to the inevitable blood bath following conquest by Hanoi? How many weeks did it take for the public to lose interest in Czechoslovakia in 1968? Who gives a damn about the millions of persecuted Christians under Communism?

Why should one now assume that public apathy about the high infant mortality rate among Aborigines is something altogether different, and proceeds from altogether different causes, i.e. "racism"? The simplest and most obvious explanation is that all these instances are symptoms of one and the same thing: not of the new-fangled disease of "white racism," but of that old and damnable selfishness which according to Christian theology is the natural state and condition of fallen human nature—black and white alike!

At least one speaker managed to interpret even the Vietnam War as an instance of Australian "racism"! I consider this absurdly far-fetched. If anything, intervention on behalf of the independence of the people of South Vietnam should have been commended as an instance of inter-racial help and understanding!

Much of what passes for "racial" conflict, may actually be more cultural or economic in nature—and should be viewed much more usefully (and

102

incidentally more calmly) as such!

To elevate race to the status of decisive, interpretative key, of a kind of universal philosophy which unlocks the real secrets of everything from bauxite to Vietnam, is not only false, in my opinion, but also highly dangerous. By focusing on the relatively minor race issue, we are likely to misunderstand and distort other, more decisive relationships, if we see them at all.

Racism and Red Herring

It strikes me as morally absurd, for instance, that little racist South Africa is widely reviled as the world's greatest evil, with which even sporting connections must be broken, while really large-scale perpetrators of crimes against humanity continue to be welcomed into the United Nations—with "anti-racist" pseudo-moralists dancing in the aisles for joy!

Christian morality surely implies a sense of proportion ("You blind guides! Straining out gnats and swallowing camels"! St. Matt. 23:24). To focus all attention on South Africa and racism, as if this were the only important moral issue, is not only immoral but dangerous: It can be used as a diversionary tactic by the forces that constitute the real threat to the freedom and well-being of people everywhere, i.e. the Marxist slave empires run from Moscow and Peking. Between the two of them these most brutal and aggressive colonial regimes of our times, both of which are publicly committed to the goal of world conquest, have killed some 100 million people. Yet there's not a peep about this from our professional moralizers—nor about the persecution of Christians today. They are all too busy denouncing South Africa—as if that little country in any way threatened the world! The objective absurdity of this topsy-turvy "morality" could hardly be greater.

Both Nazi-type racism and Marxist class-warfare would seem to be related to social Darwinism. The struggle for existence was interpreted either in terms of race or in those of class. Christianity must reject both fallacies. It certainly dare not allow itself to be prostituted into whitewashing, by silence or selectively one-eyed indignation, the greatest system of mass-murder and oppression the world has ever known!

(And while we're on the subject of moral balance, what makes the unintended infant mortality among Aboriginal Australians so much worse than the intentional infant mortality represented by legalized abortion in South Australia?)

Obsession with race is racism!

To conclude, an unbalanced obsession with race as the all-important issue does a great deal of harm to the very people who are supposed to benefit from it. Thinking Christians will not want to push the Aboriginal people of Australia into the arms of misguided, radical fanatics of the "black power" variety. Yet that is what must happen if the race-fanatics succeed in convincing everyone that race is what it's all about. To blame everything on race is a cheap excuse and an evasion of personal responsibility. After all you can do something about economics, education, culture, skills, etc., but no one can change his race or color.

There are also culturally disadvantaged, chronically poverty-stricken whites in our communities—and they are sometimes the victims of injustice at the hands of police and even courts. But they cannot cry "Racism"! To dramatize their plight and give some sort of heroic significance to their personal tragedies! I suggest that many of the problems faced by Aborigines are precisely of this sort. To evade all this with emotionally explosive catch-cries about "racism" is to compound the problem with irrational hatreds and hysterics, and thus to do a distinct disservice to the cause of Aboriginal advancement. Genuine solutions require a fair, moral, rational, and practical approach.

Is the "white racism" school of thought, with the accompanying "white devils" theory of history, any more credible or responsible than the stereotype of drunk and lazy blacks? Both are simplistic fallacies. To confirm the impression, strongly expressed in one discussion group, that it is a question of "white interest" versus "black interest," would be irresponsible lunacy in my opinion. Neither "white society" nor "black society" is that simple. Neither is a monolithic unit. Both cover a wide spectrum of differing, and conflicting—often sharply conflicting—points of view, interests, aims, methods, achievements, shortcomings, etc. No one here can speak for "the whites" or "the blacks".

I suggest that an exaggerated, obsessive preoccupation with questions of race, as if this were the all-important issue, is unrealistic, unhealthy, divisive, and counter-productive. It seems to me in fact to be itself a most undesirable, demagogic form of RACISM! I heartily agree with at least one of Kath Walker's suggestions: "Let's forget about the colors of faces, and just deal with human beings"!

K. Marquart, Lutheran minister, Member, Commission on Theology and Inter-Church Relations, Lutheran Church of Australia, and Queensland Lutheran Tertiary Education Committee. 51 Fourth Avenue Toowoomba, Qld. 4350

P.S.: These hurried, and very fragmentary observations and formulations are in no way to be regarded as an official pronouncement of my Church. They are a personal contribution to the dialogue on racism. K.M.

Christian News, July 3, 1972

1. What is the only workable opinion in our pluralistic societies? ____.
2. Any attempt to set up a "Christian" political party must ____.
3. The State must not be governed by revelation but by ____.
4. Evolutionary naturalism or scientism cannot generate ____.
5. Christians have the clear obligation of love to use the political power of citizenship in the service of ____.
6. Within the fellowship of the new humanity, racial and other

differences simply ____.

7. Can Indians be considered Christians without hearing about Christ? ____.

8. Christianity rejects other religions as ____.

9. "Social concern" is no substitute for ____.

10. Jesus taught that His kingdom ____.

11. Marxist slave empires have killed some ____.

CHURCH AND STATE:
A QUESTION OF PRINCIPLE

Luther to Hitler? In his *Ethics in a Permissive Society* (1971) William Barclay permitted himself the extraordinary remark that "Luther's ethic of church and state was the greatest disaster in all the history of ethics, for it opened the way for a kind of Christianity which allowed the state to do terrible things" (p. 188). Despite redeeming features in Luther's own ideas, said Barclay, the general impression he left was such as to lead ultimately to Hitler and his concentration camps (p. 187).

We shall not refute this silly canard here. Anyone interested in pursuing the question will find all the necessary material in a splendid article by John R. Stephenson, entitled "The Two Governments and the Two Kingdoms in Luther's Thought" *(Scottish Journal of Theology,* vol. 34 [1981] no. 4, pp. 321-337). Dr. Stephenson is now a pastor in the Missouri Synod.

THE trouble is that Lutherans themselves have become unsure of the strict distinction between spiritual and political or civil powers, even though that distinction is not Luther's personal quirk but the church's official position (*Augsburg Confession,* Arts. XVI and XXVIII). It is as if modern Lutherans were embarrassed at being found insufficiently infected with the fashionable political fever which is racking other churches—in direct proportion to their loss of doctrinal substance and stability. And so, to prove themselves as politically "responsible" as the rest, these Lutherans are busily joining together what *God,* according to their Confession, has put asunder. The coming "Evangelical Lutheran Church in America" is fully committed to political activism (see *Affirm,* August 1985). Contrary to *Augsburg Confession* XXVIII, 13: [that the spiritual authority is not to] "prescribe to civil rulers laws about the forms of government that should be established."

What is "Social Ministry"?

Onerous responses to dire human needs, such as starvation, distress caused by earthquakes and other disasters, and so on, are of course in the finest tradition of the works of mercy which have from the beginning attended the Christian faith and church. This "being a little Christ to my neighbor" (Luther), also through orphanages, hospitals, and other specialized institutions, is what "social ministry" generally means to people in the Missouri Synod. And that obviously deserves our unqualified support.

But outside the Missouri Synod "social ministry" focuses largely on something else. Consider the document, *Social Ministry Affirmation: A Challenge to Lutherans Toward the Year 1990.* The paper claims to have arisen out of "A National Assembly on Lutheran Social Ministry attended by 800 Lutherans in May 1981 in Cincinnati" and "A Consultation on Social Ministry Futures attended by 60 representatives chosen by the four church bodies and the Lutheran Council [LCUSA], meeting over a six-month period in the summer and fall of 1981."

The document lists the following among "Guiding Principles of Social Ministry": *"Analysis,* discovering what is happening in society *Education,...Service, ... Change,* helping to reform laws, systems, structures and institutions in an effort to create more justice. . ."

One of the "Societal Concerns" in the document is "reorientation of military preparedness as a means for national security and arms de-escalation."

It takes no guess-work to decode this church bureaucratese. It means simply massive political activism and propaganda in and through the churches. The general trend and direction of these political efforts is also sickeningly clear, from the record of LCUSA's own Office for Governmental Affairs in Washington, as well as from that of similar lobbies of other "ecumenical" churches.

THE allegedly prophetic utterances of the church lobbyists bear a striking family-resemblance to the sentimentalities of secular liberal make-believe. Soviet Russia must be appeased at all costs, and if the President is not willing to grovel, Congress must force disarmament on him. In Nicaragua it's "hands off." But South Africa must be punished and smashed, even if it means torturing and murdering uncooperative black civilians with barbaric "necklaces" of the Marxist controlled African National Congress!

Hunger and starvation in Africa, it is implied, are caused by Western greed and indifference, rather than by the massive mismanagement and deliberate terror imposed by Marxist regimes like the Ethiopian. There is much ado about providing "sanctuary" in American churches for alleged victims of "rightist" El Salvador, but Christian spokesmen, unlike their Jewish counterparts, hardly ever bring up the subject of millions of their co-religionists being brutally persecuted in the Soviet slave empire. That jarring topic, after all, might disrupt the sweet lullabies about "world peace"! And so it goes.

Luther was Right!

If all this proves anything, then it is surely this, that Luther was absolutely right in saying that church and state should each stick to its own affairs. The Western world's senile liberalism, which has learnt nothing in the past seventy years, could hardly have maintained such credit as it still has with the public, without the "prophetic" posturings of pseudo-religion. These emotional soap-bubbles would burst upon contact with the tough-minded common-sense justice and fairness which according to Luther (and Paul. Rom. 2:14,15; 13:1 ff!) must rule civil society.

Two examples will suffice. William Shawcross, by no means a friend of Western policy in Indo-China, has in *The Quality of Mercy shown* how Western relief supplies were withheld from the intended recipients in Cambodia, and were diverted instead to the Vietnamese occupation army, 180,000 strong! False reports of a famine were manufactured to secure funds from Western agencies.

SECONDLY why do those obsessed with South Africa never mention

Zulu Chief Buthelezi? As leader of South Africa's largest black political organization, the Inkatha movement (numbering one million members). Buthelezi opposes both the *apartheid* system and the African National Congress's (ANC) fomenting of violence. Buthelezi left the ANC in 1960, when that body turned Marxist-terrorist. Buthelezi's Inkatha "stands for the rule of law in an open, race-free society and for progress through the responsible development of free enterprise. It rejects totalitarianism etc."

Buthelezi is strongly opposed to Western economic sanctions, which he says will insure misery and violence, and ultimately dictatorship by the Moscow armed Marxist minority. He therefore scorns "prophet Tutu."

Now, is there anything in the New Testament which requires Christians as citizens to accept the politics of Tutu and to reject the politics of Buthelezi? If not, why the shrill noises in the churches? Should not such things be settled by means of informed argumentation in the political arena—outside the churches?

Closer to Home

According to the Oct. 27 *Reporter,* "Around the World," the latest issue of the Missouri Synod's *Resources for Youth Ministry,* "helps young people explore their world community..." Some of the individual items in this collection make good points (i.e., support of Lutheran World Relief), while others are simply innocuous. Taken together, however, they point in a very dubious direction, that of ecclesiastically packaged "social issues."

The effort to keep the presentations "non-political" has rendered them largely emotional, devoid of hard information. There are suggestions of the mindless poprock atmosphere, and recommended resources from churches like the LCA and the United Church of Christ, which, in the absence of clear and informed guidance, would simply render the youth more vulnerable and uncritical towards the prevailing politicized versions of all the fashionable causes.

Undoubtedly the most blatant item is the one about "peace." Here the biblical "shalom" is quickly pressed into the service of pacifist sentimentality. Students are asked to "support groups that work for peace," sign "petitions for peace," urge *"weapons freeze, nuclear disarmament, etc.,"* upon politicians, "write the President of the United States," even "put away war toys, games of violence, weapons," and "rewrite the words to 'war' hymns... 'Stand Up, Stand Up for Jesus.'... 'Lift High the Cross.'"!

The question does not even arise whether perhaps President Reagan's stand on defense endangers world peace less than would Western weakness and disarmament. Nor is there the slightest inkling that the Soviet Union might have more than a casual interest in promoting Western "peace" hysteria (see Francis Schaeffer, Vladimir Bukovsky, James Hitchcock, *Who is for Peace?).*

THIS whole trend of church-sponsored politicalization of impressionable youth should be stopped now, before it takes hold. We do not need "social issues" as our Advent (!) menu—including a litany about "injustice," which mentions South Africa and apartheid, but not one word about our fellow-Christians in the Gulag! Well-meaning but ill-informed people

108

must not be allowed to confuse the spiritual and the political domains. This is a plea not for "better politics" in the church, but for "no politics." Only in this way can the church remain faithful to her proper calling, that of distributing to mankind the precious treasures of that eternal life which "is in His Son" (I John 5:11). Experience shows that once the leaven of political passion is allowed to enter a church, it quickly becomes dominant and drives out the Gospel.

Christ himself said, "My kingship is not of this world" [St. John 18:36], and again, "Who made me a judge or divider over you?" [St. Luke 12:14]. Paul also wrote in Phil. 3:20: "Our commonwealth is in heaven," and in II Cor. 10:4,5, "The weapons of our warfare are not worldly but have divine power to destroy strongholds and every proud obstacle to the knowledge of God."

Our teachers distinguish the two authorities and the functions of the two powers, directing that both be held in honor as the highest gifts of God on earth (*Augsburg Confession,* XXVIII, 14-18).

Amen!
Prof Kurt Marquart
Concordia Theological Seminary
Ft. Wayne, Indiana
Affirm, December, 1986

Christian News, December 22, 1986

1. What did William Barclay say about Luther's ethic of Church and State? ____.
2. Did Luther lead to Hitler and his concentration camps? ____.
3. ELCA from its beginning was committed to ____.
4. What did "social ministry" mean in the LCMS? ____.
5. What did LCUSA promote? ____.
6. Who controlled the African National Congress? ____.
7. What did Buthelezi's Inkatha stand for? ____.
8. How were LCMS youth misled? ____.

SOME POINTED QUESTIONS
ABOUT HUMAN RIGHTS

Sir,—Yesterday's appeal, in your "Letters" column, on behalf of the South Africa Defense and Aid Fund, raises a number of questions. Perhaps one of the fund's supporters would care to answer them.

If March 21 has been set by the United Nations as the "International Day for the Elimination of Racial Discrimination," what day, if any has been set by that body as the "International Day for the Elimination of Communist Tyranny?"

If no such day exists, must we not conclude that in the view of the U.N., little South Africa is a greater threat to "human rights" than the Communist slave empire? By its singling out of South Africa and its silence about Communism, is not the U.N. implying perfect harmony between its "Human Rights Year" and Communism?

"Blood Bath"

Whatever may be the truth about the 1960 Sharpeville "massacre" in which 69 persons died, is it not really quite cynical to treat this, in effect, as worse than, say, the bloody suppression of the Hungarian people by Soviet troops only four years earlier? Hundreds of thousands perished there!

If the U.N. is really concerned about "human rights," why has it not to this day dared to receive and consider its own committee's report on the Hungarian blood-bath? And what about the millions of people actually slain under Communism?

If we must fuss about the claim that in South Africa, "non-whites are denied elementary political, social, and economic rights," do we not have a corresponding duty to point out that under Communism not only non-whites, but absolutely everybody except the party bosses is denied these rights, and much more brutally? Or what does the right to vote mean when only one party is allowed?

(Incidentally, while in Johannesburg last year, I was shown, not by a government agent, but by a churchman, the homes of a number of native millionaires in a native township. These successes were possible largely because the tougher white competition was kept out by law. That is the other side of "apartheid"!)

Furthermore, why ignore the known fact that in civilized countries like South Africa and Rhodesia, the native populations enjoy a far lighter standard of living than in the native-misruled countries, and that Africans are in fact fleeing to the Rhodesian and South African "police-states" from elsewhere, in search of a better way of life?

110

Hatred, Murder

Where in Africa, outside of Rhodesia and South Africa, is there any semblance of real parliamentary democracy? What are Togo, Ghana, Nigeria, Congo, Zambia, Tanzania, and the other victims of "one-man-one-vote-once," but wretched police-states? And are not the widespread tribal hatreds and massacres far worse than mere "discrimination"?

Finally, is it not true that the South Africa Defense and Aid Fund has assisted such "victims of apartheid" as Communist-linked terrorists convicted of attempting to overthrow the government by force?

In short, while as Christians we accept all Christians as brothers and all men as neighbors, many of us are sick and tired of the hypocrisy of straining out South African gnats, while swallowing the camels of Communist and African tribal atrocities.

Magnifying little injustices while in effect minimizing big ones, is itself unjust. And the frequent injections of unctuous moralisings and "Christian" rhetoric make it all the worse.

The Toowoomba Chronicle
March 21, 1968
Christian News, November 15, 1976

1. Was the Sharpville "massacre" greater than the bloody suppression of the Hungarian people? ____
2. What is the other side of apartheid? ____
3. Magnifying little injustices while in effect minimizing big ones is ____.

THE RE-CONVERSION
OF RUSSIA

Christian News, February 17, 2014
Editor's Comments - When Christian News began in 1962 who would have thought that in 2014 at the Winter Olympics in Sochi, Russia, the President of Russia would be featured as a Christian? The February 3, 2014, Washington Times published "Who's 'godless' now? Russia says it's the U.S. – Putin makes issue of traditional values." CN realizes, of course, that the Russian Orthodox Church has not always been friendly to evangelicals in Russia. Like Rome, it does not affirm the central Christian doctrine of justification by faith alone in the saving merits of Christ. Some of the hundreds of articles Christian News published opposing Communism are in the Christian News Encyclopedia. Many of them are by Kurt Marquart who fled from the Communists when they took over his native Estonia. Yet, Marquart predicted already in 1973 that there may be a re-conversion of Russia. Reprinted on p. 6 from the March 12, 1973 Christian News is "Re-Conversion of Russia by 1980" by Kurt Marquart. "Stand with Persecuted Christians" in the July 19, 1993 Christian News said after Marquart's prediction of the "Reconversion of Russia":

These Ruins Accuse

The CN editor's wife also attended the 1963 LWF Assembly as a reporter with Marquart. She was able to send CN from Finland various documents leaders of the Latvian and Estonian churches in exile had placed into the press boxes of reporters. The material placed into the press boxes by the Latvian and Estonian anti-Communists was removed by LWF officials. An announcement was then made at the LWF Assembly that no unauthorized material was to be placed into the press boxes. LWF leaders did not want the world to know what anti-Communists in Latvia and Estonia were saying. Fortunately Grace Otten got to CN's press box before the material had been removed from most press boxes. CN then was about the only church paper in the U.S. which printed what the anti-Communists Latvians and Estonians had tried to let the world know about what Communism was doing in their countries, particularly how Christians were being persecuted. CN showed that the Communist appointed churchmen praised by the LWF were lying spokesmen for the Communists. Some of the documents included pictures of churches destroyed by the Communists. (See 'These Ruins Accuse," from the Latvian National Foundation, Stockholm, Sweden, Christian News Encyclopedia, pp.509-510).

"A Tragic Day"

The August 12, l963 CN said in an editorial titled "A Tragic Day:" "It was a tragic day for Lutheranism when the Communist controlled churches of Latvia and Estonia were admitted into the Lutheran World Federation. Both the true Lutherans who are still in Latvia and Estonia and the thousands of Lutherans who have fled from these Communist na-

tions have been sadly betrayed.

"Only 13 votes were cast against the membership of these USSR churches in the LWF. U.S. Lutherans did not publicly testify against this betrayal.

'The statements made by Archbishop Jan Kiivit and Gustav Turs at The Conference of All Churches and Religious Organizations in the USS in 1952 clearly indicate that Latvia refugees are correct when they refer to these churchmen as 'Kremlin Agents.' (See "A Tragic Day")

Captive Nations Week

Christian News repeatedly urged Christian congregations to remember Captive Nations Week during the third week in July. The Unpunished Crime, by Alfred Berzins was one of the books CN recommended that pastors read as they prepared their sermon for Captive Nations Week. Berzins was elected a member of the Latvian parliament and took part in the struggle against the Soviets in 1918-1920. The Unpunished Crime tells what the Communists did to Latvia and how the Communist killed, tortured and deported Latvians. See 'The Unpunished Crime", reprinted from the June 1, 1964 CN.

Professor Kurt Marquart wrote in "The Forgotten People": (CN, January 27, 1975 CNE, 322.)

"'Remember My Chains!' (Colossians 4:18)

"When our dear Lord, in the institution of His Holy Supper, was planting the Tree of Life in the very center of His New Testament Temple, the Church, He said: 'Do this IN REMEMBRANCE of Me!'

"But He does not allow us to 'remember' Him while forgetting His people! We cannot honor the Head, if we neglect and despise His members, especially His suffering members. 'I was in prison and you came to visit Me,' Christ will say to us on Judgment Day, for 'whatever you did for one of the least of these brothers of Mine, you did for Me' (St. Matthew 25:36-40). And a stunned persecutor of 'mere people' is confronted by the God-Man Himself, demanding: 'Saul, Saul, why do you persecute ME?'(Acts 9:4).

"Fashionable Crusading

"The suffering millions, especially the Christians, in the communist slave empire are undoubtedly the world's most Forgotten People. Every little disadvantaged minority in our world receives the tender attentions of the keepers of our public conscience.

"It is quite fashionable to crusade even for the well-being of wild animals, trees, lakes, and inanimate things like burial grounds.

"But by current media manners it is OBSCENE to mention the killed and tormented millions in the Red hell. In our country people are sent to gaol for lesser cruelties to cats and dogs than are daily and routinely committed against our fellow Christians in Russia, China, and the other slave states!"

Dr. Alfred Rehwinkel and Dr. Walter Maier were among the few Lutheran theologians who recognized the threat of international Communism. They followed in the footsteps of Dr. C.F.W. Walther, first president

113

of the LCMS, who wrote in his book **Communism and Socialism**, published in 1879: *"WHY SHOULD AND CAN NO REASONABLE MAN MUCH LESS A CHRISTIAN TAKE PART IN THE EFFORTS OF COMMUNISTS AND SOCIALISTS."*

"I. Because these efforts are contrary to reason, nature, and experience . . .

"II. Because these efforts are contrary to Christianity, for . . .

"The outline of Walther's book on Communism and Socialism appears in the CN editor's Baal or God and the Christian News Encyclopedia, p. 496. Dr. Maier's views on Communism are in an appendix to Volume IV of the Christian News Encyclopedia.

When the editor was a student at Concordia Seminary, St. Louis, many of the professors and students at Concordia Seminary expressed very little interest or concern when the Communists in 1956 were killing the Hungarian Freedom Fighters. Dr. Alfred Rehwinkel was one of the few who publicly spoke up against Communism. He says in Ronald Stelzer's **Salt, Light and Signs of Times**: *"Furthermore, Russia was permitted to incorporate Latvia, Lithuania and Estonia. The people of these three Baltic countries had occupied their land for centuries; but without consideration of their rights, wishes, or lives, our democratic leaders and representatives arbitrarily surrendered them to Communism and all that implies. Then our self-proclaimed liberators and benefactors of the downtrodden agreed to permit Stalin to use prisoners of war as slave laborers in his mines and in other labor camps of Siberia and elsewhere. As a result hundreds of thousands of Germans and Japanese perished in these inhuman concentration camps, and those that returned were broken in spirit and body"* (140).

More than 20 years ago Trinity Lutheran Church of New Haven petitioned The Lutheran Church-Missouri Synod to reprint Walther's Communism and Socialism and to adopt a resolution urging that LCMS congregations remember the persecuted Christians in nations controlled by the Communists and observe Captive Nations Sunday during the third week of July as the U.S. Congress recommended in a resolution after WWII. The July 21, 1974 CN noted that LCMS President Jacob Preus was among those who signed a protesting against human rights violations for which the government of South Africa was said to be responsible. Preus said that he hoped the members of the LCMS "really get interested in this issue" of protesting against South Africa.

The January 21, 1974 CN commented: "CN has been trying for over a decade to get officials of the LCMS to express some support for Christian martyrs behind the Iron Curtain. We have thus far been unsuccessful to get them to say even a word in favor of observing Captive Nations Sunday. Officials believe it was more important for the New Orleans convention to pass resolutions supporting leftwing social issues than a resolution on Captive Nations. Why can't officials begin hoping that members of the LCMS become interested in Captive Nations Sunday and protesting the murder and slavery of Communism? Is South Africa worse than the Soviet Union?"

114

The 1975 convention of the LCMS adopted the following resolution proposed by Trinity Lutheran Church of New Haven.

(Editor's note - Kurt Marquart was the author of the major portion of this resolution)

To Stand with Persecuted Christians

WHEREAS, As Christians we are concerned about injustice and oppression wherever these are to be found; but toward our fellow Christians we have a special obligation, particularly where they are experiencing oppression in severe form; since it is well known that Christians are being more severely persecuted in territories under Communist rule; therefore be it

Resolved, That we solemnly declare our solidarity with the suffering, bleeding, yet confessing church under oppression (1 Cor. 12:16); and be it further

Resolved, That we praise God for the inspiring, victorious faith and love with which He has blest these our persecuted brethren; and be it further

Resolved, That we thank our gracious God for having hitherto preserved our nation and church from the scourge of terror and persecution; and be it finally

Resolved, That we call on all Christians who enjoy the privilege of political freedom to be well informed about the fate of Christians under oppression, to pray fervently for our persecuted fellow believers and for the conversion of their tormentors, to support these suffering Christians by every proper means, and to imitate humbly their great zeal and self-sacrifice in the service of the crucified and risen Savior; and be it further

Resolved, That we call on all church leaders to keep the cause of the oppressed Christians before world opinion and not by silence to aid and abet their persecution. We encourage them to use every proper means to do this: through the United Nations Organization, which has guaranteed the citizens basic human rights (Articles 18 and 19 of the Universal Declaration of Human Rights), urging these nations to take all steps possible to secure compliance with these declarations; through special national observances, such as Captive Nations Week; through personal leadership in their own areas to make people aware of the need for such intercession; and be it finally

Resolved, That we call on all Christians to pray for their fellow believers in the captive nations especially as a reminder to us of their needs and struggles, the same struggles with which we identify as fellow members of the body of Christ (James 5:16).

Action: Adopted (4).

(An amendment to replace "Communist" with a reference to all oppressive forms of civil government failed.)

1. At the Winter Olympics in Sochi in 2014 the President of Russia was featured as a ____.
2. What did Grace Otten find in the Christian News press box at the 1963 LWF Assembly in Helsinki? ____.
3. What was in "These Ruins Accuse?" ____.
4. Who was admitted into membership of the LWF in 1963? ____.
5. Who are "The Forgotten People?" ____?
6. What did Rehwinkel and Maier recognize? ____.
7. Who urged the LCMS to adopt a resolution calling for the recognition of Captive Nations Week? ____.
8. LCMS President Jacob Preus wanted the LCMS to protest against violations of human rights in ____.

A Marquart Prediction Twenty Years Ago

RE-CONVERSION OF RUSSIA BY 1980

Christian News, March 12, 1973
12 The Lutheran, January 29, 1973.
(Australia)

The year "1984" rings a bell with most people. But what's 1980? That will be the 1000th anniversary of the conversion of Russia to Christianity. It was in 980 that Prince Vladimir was baptized in the Dniepr River. The images of the old pagan Slavic god, Perun, were burnt and thrown into the same river.

Naturally, the present Soviet leaders are not planning any jubilee celebrations—but a lot could happen in the next eight years! Perhaps "it's time" over there!

If a re-conversion of Russia seems fantastic, consider what is happening not only in Soviet intellectual and literary life—where the greatest living Russian writer, Nobel Prize winner Alexander Solzhenitsyn, is a committed, practicing Christian—but even in the Red Army!

The amazing facts that follow are taken from an "Extraordinary Report," just to hand, addressed by the parents of a martyred Soviet soldier to the Soviet Armed Forces Minister, A.A. Grechko, to Mr. Brezhnev, to the U.N. Secretary General, and to all Christians.

Ivan Moiseyev, then 18, and a soldier in the Red Army (unit/61968 'T'), became a Christian and was baptized in 1970. For sharing the Faith with others, he was disciplined by the Army, and on July 17, 1972, his parents were informed that their son had died "tragically" on July 16. They were given the body of their son for burial in a coffin sealed with solder. The death certificate stated: "asphyxiation due to drowning."

In Ivan's home village, Volontirovka, in the Moldavian Soviet Socialist Republic, in the presence of 23 witnesses, the coffin was opened, and the body examined. According to a statement signed by all witnesses, there were six deep punctures made with a round object in the area of the heart, abrasions, burns, and other signs of torture.

Other members of their son's unit gave the parents to understand that he had been forcibly drowned after torture in order to silence his Christian witness.

End of story? Not at all! The commanding officer. Col. Malsin, an eyewitness to Ivan's death, is said to be under terrific strain, and has stated: "Moiseyev died hard, he fought with death, but he died a Christian!"

In his last letter to his parents, written only two days before his death, Ivan wrote:

"The greetings of your son will soon be at an end . . . The trials are great and the torments are not light . . . I will plant a seed and move forward . . . The commander and the soldiers say:

"There is a God. . ." After this I do not know what will follow—but

117

everything has been clear to us long ago. I wish the following for all you dear friends, young and old, just the verse of Revelation 2.10: "Be faithful unto death, and I will give you the crown of life."

"Receive these perhaps last greetings on this earth from the least of the brethren, Vanya."

No wonder the Soviet leaders are scared of Christianity! And, after all, it was through Christian "infiltration" of the Roman army that the ancient Emperor Constantine was won over! But whatever may or may not happen by 1980, one thing is sure: the future belongs to this kind of real faith—not to Marxist lies, and not to the play-religion with which many kid themselves, or the self-indulgent materialism which enslaves so much of the "Free world!"

Kurt Marquart

1. Solzhenitsyn was _____.
2. How did Ivan Moiseyev die? _____.
3. How was Emperor Constantine won over? _____.

An Excerpt From

WHEN THE WORLD WILL BE AS ONE—
The Coming New World Order
by Tal Brooke (Harvest House, 1989)

Editor's Note: These excerpts from Tal Brooke are being included in Marquart's Works since they are primarily based upon Carroll Quigley's Hope and Tragedy a book Kurt Marquart sent to the editor and urged him to study it to become better informed on what was going on in the world. He also wanted his wife, children, and others to read Hope and Tragedy.

This 300-page book is considered a classic without equal by peers in the field. It exposes the inside workings and agenda of New Age thought and the move towards a New World Order. It contains information that is mind-boggling for those with eyes to see. Since its release, it has not missed a beat in predicting the unfolding of present day events.

The Hidden Aristocracy
(An Excerpt)

The world has had an elite operating in the shadows of history and far from public view. These insiders have avoided the spotlights flooding the main stage of history. Other actors have been thrust up on stage. But the ones directing the drama have been backstage. This fractional minority of people can only activate their plans of power, and affect millions and millions of lives, if they remain out of view and beyond suspicion. It is a dangerous and risky undertaking, for they are vastly outnumbered. Secrecy is critical.

To someone who is an atheistic materialist, this idea seems preposterous. People have but one life to live, so what would inspire loyalty or sustain any participant in some grand scale conspiracy, to take over the earth, if those who finally benefited were not even on the scene for another few hundred years? How could anyone fired with ambitions for the moment be made to sacrifice his life for a long term plan? And what human channels could carry the flame of such complex and deliberate planning that spans beyond their individual lives?

The supernatural dimension is the one that gives the puzzle meaning. How else can you explain a master plan that has existed for hundreds of years? If there is a spiritual dimension guiding the insiders, a Messianic Plan, then it makes sense. Then, like a chess player who is seeing thirty moves ahead, the present sacrifice of a pawn or a rook makes perfect sense in light of the coming checkmate. Each player in the game can feel the impending victory when he manages to reach some remote crank or dial and turn it while out of public view. He becomes a cosmic player in history. He feels as if he is in the body of some corporate Messiah. He

119

can feel a kind of transnational allegiance to a higher cause, not to speak of the extremely generous temporal rewards of wealth and prestige he will usually accrue as part of the plan. And still, the lesser players in the game can continue to be motivated by the rewards of the moment. There are benefits at every level.

Almost two hundred years ago, in 1797, one of the most respected scientists in the world wrote a book entitled, PROOFS OF A CONSPIRACY (London: Creech, Cadell, Davies Publ. 1797). He was John T. Robison, Secretary General to Scotland's prestigious Royal Society and professor of natural philosophy at the University of Edinburgh. He was considered to be one of the truly great intellectuals of the day. Science was called "natural philosophy" in that day. Robison was also a high degree Mason. Whenever he travelled to Europe from Scotland, he always attended the Grand Orient Masonic Lodges. But when Robison had recently been in Europe on a sabbatical, he detected a new element in the Grand Orient Masonic Lodges. More than that, Adam Weishaupt, the founder of these new elite, approached Robison to join an inner circle. It was known as Illuminism. It was the quiet flame that burned in the French intelligentsia such as Voltaire, Robespierre, Mirabeau, and the Duc D'Orleans.

The Illuminist plan was to unseat the present powers of hereditary aristocracy and replace it with an intellectual aristocracy, using a staged revolt of the masses to do this. This, indeed, was exactly what the French Revolution appeared to be, key people catalyzing great numbers of people.

Robison warned the royal family of England that hidden powers were pulling strings. That the French Revolution was not a historical accident happening by whim but that it was manipulated by geniuses who had their own agenda. There was one genius in particular behind Illuminism.

Like Karl Marx, he was of Jewish descent, but had temporarily joined the Jesuit Order.

Later he got into league with some powerful German merchants who were initiates in the occult. Adam Weishaupt was a professor of Canon Law at the University of Ingolstadt. He started the Order of the Illumination May 1, 1776. His plan was to use the Grand Orient Lodges of Europe as a filtering mechanism through which to screen out talent and build a hierarchy of inner circles. Like the Mafia of today, only the inner inner circle could be trusted with the true purpose of the Order.

The true purpose of the Illuminati, according to professor Robison, was world hegemony, a world order ruled by an elite pretending to represent the common man: An elite who had penetrated into every aspect of society from the arts to politics and law while shaping public opinion with more subtlety than the average citizen was able to detect. Weishaupt's plan involved a communistic order outlined a full seventy years before Marx came on the scene.

But Weishaupt was exposed in 1785 when the Bavarian government stepped in and seized his papers. An unknown variable had caused exposure. The hidden hand was forced to come out of the shadows for a mo-

120

ment. The horseman, named Lanze, carrying various secret papers and plans to France, was struck and killed by lightning in Regensberg. The local police handed the papers over to the Bavarian government. Then when the Bavarian government questioned four professor colleagues of Weishaupt, they testified to the conspiracy. On historical record is the attempt of the Bavarian government to warn other European governments in an official document entitled, *Original Writings of the Order and Sect of the Illuminati.* Four years after lightning struck the horseman, the French Revolution rocked Europe.

Rumor remained that the Illuminati then shifted locations to Italy calling itself "the invisible forty." By the early 1800's Weishaupt and his conspiratorial Illuminists were mentioned in the correspondence of George Washington, Jefferson, Madison, and John Quincy Adams. They did not want this plan infiltrating America any more than Robison wanted to see it in England. They had seen the ruthlessness of France's "Reign of Terror." George Washington wrote in 1798: "It is not my intention to doubt that the doctrine of the Illuminati and the principles of Jacobinism had not spread in the United States. On the contrary, no one is more satisfied of this fact than I am." [THE WRITINGS OF GEORGE WASHINGTON, published by the U.S. Government Printing Office, 1941, vol. 20, p. 518] That was two hundred years ago. And indeed a connecting thread existing through the 1800's. It had to do with merchant bankers, occultists, as well as other invisible players.

200 Years Later

Today, the power of a certain group of bankers is colossal according to Harvard and Princeton Professor Emeritus, Carroll Quigley, who confessed to being an insider and confidant of this elite group. Professor Quigley's **magnum opus**, TRAGEDY AND HOPE: A HISTORY OF OUR TIME, rocked those who saw it when it came out in 1966. This 1,300-page book named major insider power groups attempting to manipulate a world socialist order. Quigley ardently supported the plan but said that it should no longer be under cover. His book was a triumphalist announcement of the inevitable since the plan had virtually reached completion. He had been among the intellectual brain trust rubbing shoulders with the insiders. The problem was that he had said too much. The Macmillan first edition of 1966 suddenly disappeared almost overnight, even from public libraries.

Copies were removed. When Professor Quigley took his final academic post and taught at the Georgetown University School of Foreign Service, an acquaintance of mine in the sixties took every class under Doctor Quigley that he could enroll in and spoke of this Ivy League professor in almost messianic language.

When I got a copy of Quigley's book, TRAGEDY AND HOPE, printed in Taiwan (an exact copy of the original Macmillan book which my friend owned) I was amazed. Indeed, Professor Quigley had let too much out of the bag. That book and others, twelve years ago, opened a cryptic doorway. It enabled me to glimpse the reality of some of the elite insiders manipulating world events in order for their plan to take shape. The reality of what was happening was even more incredible than Robert Ludlum's MATARESE CIRCLE. Here finally was tangible evidence of insiders who were so well versed at removing their own fingerprints that they slipped detection. Evidence had previously come in faint traces here and there. Certain names kept cropping up. When author Ian Flemming, who for years had been a member of the British Secret Service, wrote about James Bond combating such secret conspiratorial groups as SMERSH and SPECTER, one wonders whether he was indulging in more than just fiction? Showing insider's knowledge thinly veiled? According to Quigley, yes, such hidden groups most certainly do exist. And they are beautifully camouflaged. The average person would not think twice as their stretch limousines with tinted windows glide down Park avenue or London's Bond street.

Harvard Professor emeritus Quigley divulges the following about this "international network" in TRAGEDY AND HOPE: ". . . this network which we may identify as the Round Table Groups, has no aversion to cooperating with the Communists or any other group, and frequently does so. I know of the operations of this network because I have studied it for twenty years and was permitted for two years, in the early 1960's, to examine its papers and secret records. I have no aversion to it or to most of its aims and have, for much of my life, been close to it and to many of its instruments." [Carroll Quigley, TRAGEDY AND HOPE, (New York: the Macmillan Company, 1966 p. 950)] In the next sentence, Quigley only differs on one point with the insider network, "It wishes to remain unknown." Other sources have led me to believe that Quigley went very deep, but that there are things even deeper.

Quigley summarizes the insider's Grand Plan: "Their aim is nothing less than to create a WORLD SYSTEM of financial control in private hands able to dominate the political system of each country and the economy of the world as a whole. The system was to be controlled in a feudalistic fashion by the CENTRAL BANKS OF THE WORLD ACTING IN CONCERT, by secret agreements arrived at in frequent private meetings and conferences." [Ibid., p. 324.] This is almost a perfect description of the secret international meetings of—the Bilderbergers—"secret agreements arrived at in frequent private meetings. . ."

One fact that Quigley and others reveal is that the banking houses owned by the great family dynasties are also the banks behind the International Monetary Fund as well as the World Bank. The same names keep cropping up. They are king makers and nation breakers. The goal is a global central bank once national banks have been established and conditions are right.

So far, the central banking system projected for Europe in 1992 is a major milestone to this goal. And not a small part of this gradualist agenda is America's own central bank, the Federal Reserve Bank. So is national debt highly in their favor. The two trillion dollars now owed to them by the United States, as they wear the outer attire of the Federal Reserve Bank, gives this inner circle of select banks yearly interest payments of over one hundred billion dollars. Elections and stock markets can switch directions overnight with a directive from the Federal Reserve. Alan Greenspan, the visible chairman of the Federal Reserve, could change the prime lending rate and cause a panic, a recession, indeed, a depression with a single word. The politician that does the bidding of the insiders gets in the door. It is always good policy to justify substantial loans from these banks. The rhetoric is irrelevant and has been for a very long time. Just watch one president after another promise to balance the national debt, then watch it quietly climb off the graph. The debt will soon equal the sum total assets of the nation. How do banks and money barons manipulate conditions?

According to Harvard economist, John Kenneth Galbraith, Winston Churchill was shown an interesting object lesson by New York banker and industrial magnate Bernard Baruch in 1929. Baruch was an advisor to President Wilson at the treaty of Versailles, beside that other great advisor, "Colonel" Mandel House. Baruch also advised Roosevelt and was a member of his brain trust. During World War One, Baruch, when he was Chairman of the War Industries Board, made hundreds of millions of dollars from lucrative contracts in the war and munitions industry. He was at the right place at the right time. According to the Harvard economist Galbraith, Baruch walked Sir Winston Churchill out on the floor of the New York Stock exchange the morning it fell. [John Kenneth Galbraith, THE GREAT CRASH, 1929, (New York: Time Inc., 1954), p. 102] Churchill was brought to witness the crash firsthand on October 24, 1929, because it was desired that he see the power of the banking system at work. This presumes plenty of lead time for Winston to take the ship from England to the United States, hang out for a while, maybe start the day with a good breakfast at the Waldorf and make it there in time to see the floor open up. This is insider knowledge that would pale Simon Boesky's. We will see later why Baruch gave Churchill this object lesson.

The American market collapsed that day of 1929 and so did the world market not long after. Economic conditions for the next world war were set up, greatly aided by America's Great Depression. Billions of dollars shifted hands overnight. Some had gotten out in time, the big hitters, while scores of the wealthy were destroyed. Then, after the Crash, when railroads and industries plummeted, the big hitters came back on the stock market floor and bought industries at whim for a dime on the dollar. One such "fortunate speculator" was Bernard Baruch who had boasted to Churchill that he had liquidated his stock holdings when the market was at the top and bought bonds, gold, while retaining a huge cash reserve. Now he could buy companies like pieces on a monopoly board. Millions of lives were wrecked and America suddenly needed a "New Deal" in the form of social welfare. The Great Crash created another precedent for free America, gradual socialism, as the Fabians had been doing in England. Why would any banker or insider be the least bit attracted to socialism? Because the idea that socialism is a share-the-wealth program is strictly a confidence game to get the people to surrender their freedom to an all-powerful collective. It is a means to consolidate and control wealth. Once this is understood it is no longer a paradox that the super-rich promote it. Here is another riddle, once the central banks become "socialized," as in Britain, the ownership remains the same. Rothschild still controls the Bank of England, and the Bank of England is still a private bank. And as a central bank, it is literally above the law.

While wars and revolutions have been useful to international bankers in gaining or increasing control over governments, the key to such control has always been control of money. You can control a government if you have it in your debt. A creditor can demand special privileges from the sovereign. Money seeking governments have granted monopolies in state banking, along with natural resources, oil concessions, etc. But the monopoly that the international bankers most covet is control over a nation's money. The famed quote of Lord Rothschild to his friend Benjamin Disraeli, England's first Jewish Prime Minister, was—"As long as I control a nation's currency, I care not who makes its laws." Disraeli's novel CONINGSBY, a thinly veiled story that involved Rothschild, contained the following interesting quote: 'The world is governed by very different personages from what is imagined by those who are not behind the scenes." [Benjamin Disraeli, CONINGSBY, p. 233.) This is true.

International bankers actually own as private companies the central banks of the key European nations. The Bank of England, Bank of France, and Bank of Germany are not owned by their respective governments, as most people imagine, but are privately owned monopolies that were granted by the heads of state. That is precisely why the *London Financial Times* of Sept. 26, 1921, revealed that even at the time, "Half a dozen men at the top of the Big Five Banks could upset the whole fabric of government finance by refraining from renewing Treasury Bills."

But Professor Quigley revealed that these visible heads at the top of the Big Five Banks were only front men, the *agentur* of the invisible international bankers. Again, it was imperative that the shadow figures stay in the shadows and work behind front men. Quigley directly addresses the issue of the front men of the State Banks of Europe:

"It must not be felt that these heads of the world's chief central banks were themselves substantive powers in world finance. They were not. Rather, they were the technicians and agents of the dominant investment bankers of their own countries, who had raised them up and were perfectly capable of throwing them down. The substantive financial powers of the world were in the hands of these investment bankers (also known as 'international' or 'merchant bankers') who remained largely behind the scenes in their own unincorporated private banks. These formed a system of international cooperation and national dominance which was more private, more powerful, and more secret than that of *their agents* in the central banks." [Carroll Quigley, TRAGEDY AND HOPE, pp. 326-327.]

Such a front man was Montagu Norman who was Governor of the Bank of England. He suddenly came to America the year of the Great Crash, in February of 1929 to confer with Andrew Mellon, the Secretary of the Treasury. *The Wall Street Journal* on November 11, 1927 had al ready referred to Norman as "the currency dictator of Europe." Wrong. He was the front man for Lord Rothschild, the true currency dictator of Europe. Norman, a close friend of JP Morgan, had said of himself, "I hold the hegemony of the world," according to Dr. Quigley. John Hargrave who wrote the biography about and entitled MONTAGU NORMAN, cited the dream of this titular head of the Bank of England: "that the Hegemony of world Finance should reign supreme over everyone, everywhere, as one whole supernational control mechanism." [John Hargrave, MONTAGU NORMAN (New York: Greystone Press, 1942)] Norman was parroting someone else's view behind the scenes. The Fabian Society of Britain, another of Quigley's inner circle round table groups who were present at Versailles, had worked up the gradualist agenda for the spread of socialism.

Americans needed the back door approach. So after the crash, which in turn started the Great Depression, in came the Trojan horse of socialism in its first small increments as Roosevelt was cast in the light of the savior of the people with welfare and government programs. Not far behind were his liberal advisors, including Mr. Baruch who had also advised President Woodrow Wilson (having contributed generously to both Wilson's and Roosevelt's campaigns). Take note that within a decade of Churchill's object lesson on the floor, he became one of Britain's greatest prime ministers. His bid as prime minister had failed repeatedly. But with the right support, he was elected.

Creating America's Central Bank

How did America finally get a Central Bank like its European cousins? Let's look back again. There were numerous attempts in the 1800's to create a central bank in America. Most of these attempts point back to the Rothschilds.

The Rothschilds had their invisible hands in many of the early major American banking houses. One banker was August Belmont, a superstar of Birmingham's OUR CROWD (whose original family name was Schoenberg). He used to put ads in the New York paper advertising himself as Rothschild's agent. He became incredibly wealthy. In the South, Rothschild had the Erlangers.

It is interesting that both the original American banking houses that represented Rothschild, August Belmont and the Erlangers, funded the North and the South respectively during America's Civil War. Rothschild sent August Belmont to the United States during the Panic of 1837 and empowered him to buy government bonds. Right then the Civil War started. Whichever side won owed its respective banker for the victory. Could the goal be monopoly of capital?

It seems Abraham Lincoln saw the power play behind this masquerade as one bank was seemingly played against the other. The invisible hand underneath was never seen by the multitudes. Lincoln did see it, for he had resisted the pressure to create in America a central private bank that would print its money. He also spotted the "divide and conquer" movement where the North was pitted against the South with both sides financed by the same money elite.

Abraham Lincoln battled for the right of Congress and the Treasury to hold the awesome power of coining money. He knew that to surrender his power to private banks was ultimately to surrender the sovereignty of America. Adams and Jefferson had warned of this all along. Defying the hidden bankers, Lincoln issued the greenbacks. Then Lincoln was assassinated.

Forty years later, there was another event. John Pierpont Morgan created the panic of 1907 and was amply rewarded. He gained numerous holdings as well as his bid to be the Rothschild's number one American agent. J. P. Morgan's real feat, and service to Rothschild, in the Panic of 1907, was that he created a mood in America that was receptive to a central bank to be known as the Federal Reserve Bank. Morgan's own bank, The Morgan Guaranty Trust, was allowed to be among the inner circle of primary owners of the Fed. It is interesting that Morgan had spent five months in Europe right before the 1907 Panic shuttling between London and Paris. He was gaining an inside look at Europe's central banks.

The New York Times, Oct. 26, 1907, noted in connection with J. P. Morgan's actions during the Panic of 1907, "In conversation with the *New York Times* correspondent. Lord Rothschild paid a high tribute to J.P. Morgan for his efforts in the present financial juncture in New York. 'He is worthy of his reputation as a great financier and a man of wonders. His latest action fills one with admiration and respect for him.'" This is the only time a Rothschild praised another banker outside his own family. A few decades later, the *New York Times* dropped another nugget. On March 28, 1932, during the Great Depression, the *New York Times* noted, "London: N.M. Victor Rothschild, twenty-one-year-old nephew of Baron Rothschild, is going to the United States soon to take a post with J.P. Morgan & Co., it was learned tonight."

Soon after J .P. Morgan had created the Panic of 1907, the American people were in the right mood to believe that a central bank would prevent such a panic from occurring again. When the moment was right, Senator Aldrich, who later married into the Rockefeller family when his daughter Abbey married John D. Rockefeller, Jr., was in place to push through the Federal Reserve Act. That delicate moment was during a lame duck Senate, right before the Christmas break, on Dec. 22, 1913. Immediately before that, Aldrich, representing the Rockefellers, with Paul Warburg, who represented the Rothschild's as well as Kuhn Loeb, had gone to Jeckyl Island, Georgia in a sealed train, away from the press, to iron out how they would present the Federal Reserve Bill to the House and Senate. Paul Warburg was the banking genius who understood the labyrinthine structure of the Federal Reserve Bank. And Aldrich was the PR man in the Senate.

Warburg had some interesting connections. Paul Warburg had come to America ten years prior, in 1902, from the Warburg Bank of Germany. He married Nina Loeb, daughter of Kuhn Loeb founder Solomon Loeb, while his brother, Felix, married Frieda Schiff, the daughter of Jacob Schiff, who was head of Kuhn Loeb. Jacob Schiff was the ruling power of

Kuhn Loeb. Both Paul and Felix were made full partners of Kuhn Loeb. And Paul was finally paid an annual salary of half a million dollars (then!) to enlighten the public on the need for a central bank. His father-in-law, who paid him his colossal salary to set up the Federal Reserve, was Jacob Schiff. Stephen Birmingham writes in his authoritative best-seller, OUR CROWD: THE GREAT JEWISH FAMILIES OF NEW YORK: "In the eighteenth century the Schiffs and Rothschilds shared a double house" in Frankfurt. Jacob Schiff reportedly bought his partnership into Kuhn Loeb with Rothschild money. Hence the Kuhn Loeb connection with Rothschild.

Once Senator Aldrich had gotten the Federal Reserve Act through the Senate, Woodrow Wilson, under the nod from "Colonel" Mandel House, signed the Federal Reserve Act. Among the international financiers who contributed heavily to the Woodrow Wilson's campaign were Jacob Schiff, Bernard Baruch, Henry Morgenthau and *New York Times* publisher Adolph Ochs. Insider banker Bernard Baruch was later made absolute dictator over American business when President Wilson appointed him Chairman of the War Industries Board, where he had control of all domestic contracts for Allied war materials. Hence his war industries profits of over two hundred million dollars.

—End of excerpt from WHEN THE WORLD WILL BE AS ONE: the coming new world order by Tal Brooke (Harvest House, 1989).

* * *

Tal Brooke is president of Spiritual Counterfeits Project (SCP), a nationwide ministry. Box 4308, Berkeley, CA 94704. He spent two decades intently exploring the occult. His quest ultimately landed him in the heart of India where for two years he was the top western disciple of India's miracle-working super guru, Saf Baba. A graduate of the University of Virginia, and Princeton, and a frequent speaker at Oxford and Cambridge Universities, Tal has written four books including his biography, *Avatar of Night*, which is a bestseller in India.

Christian News, January 30, 1995

1. John T. Robinson is the author of ____.
2. Robinson was a high degree ____.
3. Who was Adam Weishaupt? ____.
4. The Illuminist plan was to ____.
5. What did George Washington say about the Illuminati? ____.
6. Quigley ardently supported ____ but said it should no longer be ____.
7. What happened to Macmillan's first edition of *Tragedy and Hope*? ____.
8. Round Table Groups have no aversion to cooperating with ____.

9. The Grand Plan of the insiders is to ____.
10. Who are the Bilderbergers? ____.
11. Who are the banks behind the International Monetary Fund? ____.
12. Who was Bernard Baruch? ____.
13. Wars and revolutions have been useful to ____.
14. You can control a government if ____.
15. What did Benjamin Disraeli say? ____.
16. Montaga Norman was ____.
17. What started the Great Depression? ____.
18. Who funded both the North and South during the Civil War? ____.
19. J.P. Morgan's great feat was ____.

When The World Will Be One—The Coming New
World Order

GIVE TAL BROOKE A HEARING—WHO WILL REFUTE HIM?

The excerpt in this issue, p. 1, from **When The World Will Be One—The Coming New World Order** by Tal Brooke deserves a careful hearing. Some 40 years ago we read many books on what some refer to as "conspiracies," books about the Free Masons, the Illuminati, Council of Foreign Relations, the Trilateralists, the International Bankers, the Communists, the Zionists, Bilderbergers, etc. As a young student, we were determined to learn the truth and did not limit our reading to books recommended by our professors.

Tal Brooke mentions Dr. Carroll Quigley's **Tragedy and Hope—A History of the World in Our Time,** first published by MacMillan in 1966. Quigley was one of President Bill Clinton's professors at Georgetown. The August 16, 1971 Christian News published a review of W. Cleon Skousen's **The Naked Capitalist,** which is a commentary on Quigley's much larger work **(Christian News Encyclopedia,** p. 304). Professor Kurt Marquart gave us a copy of Quigley's **Tragedy and Hope.** We noted in a review of this 1,348-page book, which has been difficult to obtain: "One need not agree with everything in **Tragedy and Hope** to admire the author's tremendous knowledge of the world in our time. The Christian, of course, should always recognize that throughout history there is the struggle between the forces of Christ and Satan. At various times in history Satan uses various destructive forces to carry out his sinister purposes."

"**Tragedy and Hope** belongs in at least every college library. History professors should consider it for possible textbook use. They should by all means read the book themselves."

Anthony Sutton's **Wall Street and the Bolshevik Revolution** (New Rochelle, Arlington House, 1974, $7.95.) Reviewed in the October 14, 1974 CN) is a good book to study along with **Tragedy and Hope.** Sutton in his important book shows that there is a definite link between some New York bankers and many revolutionaries, including the Bolsheviks. **Christian News Encyclopedia,** p. 304.

"An Invitation to Refute Quigley, Sutton, Skousen— CONSPIRACY THEORY REVIVED," an editorial in the April 26, 1982 **Christian News,** noted in part: "**Human Events** reports that a posthumous book by the late Georgetown University professor Dr. Carroll Quigley is now available under the title: **The Anglo-American Establishment: The Conspiracy From Rhodes to Clivendon.**"

"**Tragedy and Hope** shows that some of the richest people in the world support Communism and Socialism." "We recognize that the lu-

129

natic fringe has come up with all sorts of weird conspiratorial theories. We have been sent much of their literature for over twenty years. But the work of such scholars as Quigley, Sutton, and Skousen cannot be so easily shrugged off as the unsupported wild notions of right wing kooks.

"Liberal churchmen, who generally maintain that they are far better informed about world affairs than orthodox theologians, who they say are only interested in doctrine, should attempt to refute Quigley's **Tragedy and Hope,** Skousen's **The Naked Capitalist,** and Sutton's **Wall Street and The Bolshevik Revolution.** If a liberal churchman sends us an article refuting these books, which have received favorable publicity in Christian News, we'll publish it. Let's get the facts out on the table."

No one sent CN any article or letter which attempted to refute Quigley, Skousen and Sutton.

CN now extends the same offer to anyone who wants to refute Tal Brooke's **When the World Will Be One— The Coming New World Order,** particularly what Tal Brooke writes in the excerpt appearing in this issue of CN.

Christian News, January 30, 1995

1. Some of the conspiracies are books about ____.
2. President ____ had Dr. Caroll Quigley as a professor at George town University.
3. A good book to study along with **Tragedy and Hope** is ____.
4. **Tragedy and Hope** shows that some of the richest people in the world support ____.

A Gift From Kurt Marquart

QUIGLEY'S
TRAGEDY AND HOPE

"Fed Bankers Seek Power More Than Wealth," reproduced here from the January 4, 2010 *The New American,* is one of the books LCMS Professor Kurt Marquart presented to this editor as a gift. He was always trying to keep CN informed about many matters. When the editor and Marquart were roommates, they discussed many subjects besides theology, as inquisitive youths will . They even experimented with extra-sensory perception.

The New American says that "Professor Carroll Quigley's 1966 opus *Tragedy and Hope* contains many important revelations. He bared the existence of a secret society that planned to rule the world even naming the Council of Foreign Relations as its American branch."

E. L. Hebden Taylor in his perceptive *Christian Reflections Upon New Revelations About The Second World War-- Who Really Started World War Two and When Did It Begin?* (*Christian News Encyclopedia,* pp. 4180-4185) mentions Quigley's *Tragedy and Hope.* Reproduced here from the October 9, 1989 Christian News (CNE, 5447) is *"Tragedy or Hope"* by P.H. vanderWerff, a well informed Canadian lay theologian who wrote many articles opposing millennialism. The April 26, 1982 Christian News published "An Invitation to Refute Quigley, Sutton, Skousen--Conspiracy Theory Revived." *The Christian News Encyclopedia* includes vital information about hundreds of subjects and thousands of names. All five volumes are available from CN for $52.52. What Christian News said in its review of Quigley's great work CN still says. Those who want to be informed about world affairs should read it (CN, December 18, 1978). CN said:

***Tragedy and Hope -- A History Of The World In Our Time.* By Carroll Quigley. First published in 1966 by The MacMillan Company, New York--Collier-MacMillan Limited, London. Second Printing, 1974 by W. Morrison. Order from Angriff Press, Box 2726, Hollywood, California 90028. 1348 pages.**

Although this book was first published by one of the world's leading publishers and written by one of the most learned historians of our day, it has been largely ignored by the mass media and copies are now extremely difficult to obtain. It is no longer available from MacMillan. Recently one of our professors sent us a copy and told us where it was available.

We have for some time been familiar with Cleon Skouson's *The Naked Capitalist,* which summarizes much of the book. Seven years ago we published a review of *The Naked Capitalist,* which appeared in the Roman Catholic *The Wanderer.* We are again reprinting the review.

Quigley's book gives a picture of the world in terms of the influence of different cultures and outlooks upon each other; it shows, more completely than in any similar work, the influence of science and technology on human life; and it explains, with unprecedented clarity, how the intricate financial and commercial patterns of the West prior to 1914 influenced the development of today's world.

The author writes that "The merchant bankers of London had already at hand in 1810-1850 the Stock Exchange, the Bank of England, and the London money market when the needs of advancing industrialism called all of these into the industrial world which they had hitherto ignored. In time they brought into their financial network the provincial banking centers, organized as commercial banks and saving banks, as well as insurance companies, to form all of these into a single financial system on an international scale which manipulated the quantity and flow of money so that they were able to influence, if not control, governments on one side and industries on the other. The men who did this, looking backward toward the period of dynastic monarchy in which they had their own roots, aspired to establish dynasties of international bankers and were at least as successful at this as were many of the dynastic political rulers. The greatest of these dynasties, of course, were the descendants of Meyer Amschel Rothschild (1743-1812) of Frankfort, whose male descendants, for at least two generations, generally married first cousins or even nieces. Rothschild's five sons, established at branches in Vienna, London, Naples, and Paris, as well as Frankfort, cooperated together in ways which other international banking dynasties copied but rarely excelled" (51).

Baring, Lazard, Erlanger, Warburg, Schroeder, Seligman, the Speyers, Mirabaud, Fould, and Morgan are other banking families mentioned by Quigley. He notes that "these bankers were almost equally devoted to secrecy and the secret use of financial influence in political life. These bankers came to be called 'international bankers' and, more particularly, were known as 'merchant bankers' in England, 'private bankers' in France, and 'investment bankers' in the United States." He adds that "This persistence as private firms continued because it ensured the maximum of anonymity and secrecy to persons of tremendous public power who dreaded public knowledge of their activities as an evil almost as great as inflation" (52). The author claims that "On the whole, in the period up to 1931, bankers, especially the Money Power controlled by the international investment bankers, were able to dominate both business and government" (60).

Professor Quigley writes: "In addition to their power over government based on government financing and personal influence, bankers could steer governments in ways they wished them to go by other pressures. Since most government officials felt ignorant of finance, they sought advice from bankers whom they considered to be experts in the field. The history of the last century shows, as we shall see later, that the advice given to governments by bankers, like the advice they gave to industrialists, was consistently good for bankers ,but was often disastrous for governments, businessmen, and the people generally. Such advice could be enforced if necessary by manipulation of exchanges, gold flows, discount rates, and even levels of business activity. Thus Morgan dominated Cleveland's second administration by gold withdrawals, and in 1936-1938 French foreign exchange manipulators paralysed the Popular Front governments. As we shall see, the powers of these antenatal bankers reached their peak in the last decade of their supremacy, 1919-1931, when Montagu Norman and J.P. Morgan dominated not only the financial world but international relations and other matters as well" (62).

Quigley's book can't be chalked off as the rantings of some rapid anti-Communist extremist. Here is what he says about Senator Joseph R. McCarthy: "McCarthy was not a conservative, still less a reactionary. He was a fragment of elemental force, a throwback to primeval chaos. He was the enemy of all order and of all authority, with no respect, or even understanding, for principles, laws, regulations, or rules. As such, he had nothing to do with rationality or generality. Concepts, logic, distinctions of categories were completely outside his world if it is, for example, perfectly clear that he did not have any idea of what a communist was, still less of communism itself, and he did not care. . ." (928-929).

One need not agree with everything in Tragedy and Hope to admire the author's tremendous knowledge of the world in our time. The Christian, of course, should always recognize that throughout history there is the struggle between the forces of Christ and Satan. At various times in history Satan uses different sinister forces to carry out his destructive purposes. The book's jacket notes that "Carroll Quigley, professor of history at the Foreign Service School of Georgetown University, formerly taught at Princeton and at Harvard. He has done research in the archives of France, Italy, and England, and is the author of the widely praised Evolution of Civilizations. A member of the editorial board of the monthly Current History, he is a frequent lecturer and consultant for public and semi-public agencies."

Tragedy & Hope belongs in at least every college library. History professors should consider it for possible text book use. They should by all means read the book themselves.

Anthony Sutton's Wall Street and the Bolshevik Revolution (New Rochelle, New York: Arlington House, 1974. $7.95. Reviewed in the October 14, 1974 CN) is a good book to study along with Tragedy & Hope. Sutton in his important book shows that there is a definite link between some New York bankers and many revolutionaries, including Bolsheviks. This prominent scholar writes: "We find there was a link between some New York international bankers and many revolutionaries, including Bolsheviks. These banking gentlemen--who are here identified -- had a financial stake in, and were rooting for the success of the Bolshevik Revolution

"Who, why--and for how much--is the story in this book" (11).

1. What did The New American say about Carroll Quigley's Hope and Tragedy? _____.
2. Who first published Hope and Tragedy? _____.
3. Who are some of the banking families mentioned by Quigley? _____.
4. According to Quigley who was able to dominate both business and government? _____.
5. Throughout history there has been a struggle between the forces of _____.
6. What did Anthony Sutton say in Wall Street and the Bolshevik Revolution? _____.

AGENDA – GRINDING AMERICA DOWN

Those who maintain that Communism is now dead should watch this DVD of some two hours. Anyone who thinks *Christian News* is out of date by now publishing a volume in *Marquart's Works* series on Communism and Socialism should carefully listen to what many of the leading anti-Communist scholars have to say in this DVD.

Before *Christian News* began, such films as *My Latvia* and J. Edgar Hoover's *Masters of Deceit* were shown in many anti-Communist study groups, including the editor's congregation, where Kurt Marquart spoke.

Grinding America Down

The editor had learned about them at a conference in St. Louis in 1958 of Fred Schwarz's Christian anti-Communist organization Marquart championed. Schwarz had come from Australia. Cleon Skousen, the author of the *Naked Capitalist*, mentioned in *Agenda* often lectured with Schwarz. *The Naked Capitalist* is a good introduction to Carroll Quigley's monumental *Tragedy and Hope* first published by McMillan and recommended by Kurt Marquart.

Agenda – Grinding America Down is dedicated to Fred Schwarz. It features such Anti-Communists often recommended in *Christian News* as John Stormer, Phyllis Schlafly, David Noebel, M. Stanton Evans, Ed Meese, Branson Howes and others.

Fred Schwarz was instrumental in the formation of many anti-Communist study groups across America. This editor attended the meetings of one of these groups in the home of Dr. and Mrs. Harry Sammons in Kirkwood, Missouri. They were great supporters of the work of Fred Schwarz. There the editor first met John Stormer, the author of *None Dare Call It Treason* which eventually was published in some 7 million copies. Kurt Marquart noted that intellectual snobs do not even acknowledge the existence of facts in books like Stormer's *None Dare Call It Treason* with which they disagree.

After thanking some 40 publishers for permission to use their copyrighted material, the "Acknowledgements" in the editor's *Baal or God* published in 1965 says "While the author alone is to be held responsible for the content of this book, special thanks are due to Siegbert W. Becker, Harold W. Romoser, Paul H. Burgdorf, Kenneth K. Miller, William H. Bischoff, and John H. Stormer for reading a major portion of the manuscript and for making helpful suggestions; to James Bales, John Whitcomb, Henry Morris, and Edgar C. Bundy for offering helpful suggestions on various chapters..."

Stormer came to New Haven to give *Christian News* some advice on publishing an inexpensive paperback. Stormer and the editor attended the Sixth Congress of the International Council of Churches in Geneva, Switzerland where a copy of *Baal or God* was placed by the anti-communist International Council of Christian Churches into the registration packet of each delegate. They came from more than a hundred nations and several hundred denominations. *Baal or God* has a chapter on Communism, the Law of God, and America's Moral Revolution, Sexplosion, Homosexuality, Standards of Right and Wrong, etc.

CN first met David Noebel when the editor was invited to speak at a Christian Crusade conference for pastors held in Tulsa, Oklahoma when Noebel was still with Christian Crusade. This group ordered a thousand copies of *CN*'s *Baal or God*.

CN has often promoted the fine anti-communist and educational work of Phyllis Schlafly who appears several times on *Agenda-Grinding America Down*. The editor had just recently graduated from Concordia Seminary, St. Louis when she called him to have the invocation at one of her well attended rallies. *CN* was asked by anti-Communist Church League of America leaders to enter full time anti-Communist work at a good salary. The editor opted to remain the pastor of Trinity, New Haven which he had begun serving as a graduate student.

Representative Curtis Bowers and the producers of *Agenda – Grinding American Down* clearly show what is happening to American youth, the danger of the rise of homosexuality and that Communism and Socialism remain a threat. The DVD shows that the publication of Volume II of *Marquart's Works* on Communism is so important today. Don't expect official denominational publications, the sacerdotalists and organized conservatives to mention *Agenda – Grinding America Down* no more than they ever mentioned *Baal or God*, or any publication of *Christian News*, including Beck's An American Translation of the Bible, the most accurate translation of the Bible in the Language of Today. *Agenda – Grinding America Down* defends the Bible.

Some other anti-Communists and supporters of free enterprise and Christian or home schools interviewed are Jim Simpson, Trevol Lauden, Janet Porter, H.L. Richardson, Robert Chandler, Howard Philips, Bryan Fischer, Beverly Eakman, Mike Smith, E. Calvin Beiser, Cliff Kincaid, Tim Wildman, Mary Wright, and others.

Among those whose socialistic and anti-Christian views are exposed are Stalin, Lenin, Hitler, Barack Obama, Saul Alinsky, George Bernard Shaw, John Dewey, Better Frieden, and Jim Wallis of Sojourners.

The Mattachine Society is exposed. This group is mentioned in the section on Homosexuals in *CN*'s *Baal or God*.

Agenda – Grinding America Down should be shown not only at gatherings of such conservative groups as the Lutheran Concerns Association (p. 1) but in homes, churches and colleges across America. Often conservatives when they meet do little more than meet, eat, and retreat. *Agenda – Grinding America Down* is a good DVD to promote congregational study and positive action.

For information see www.agendadocumentary.com

Christian News, September 22, 2014

1. Who was Fred Schwarz? ____.
2. Cleon Skousen wrote ____.
3. Carroll Quigley wrote ____.
4. What did Kurt Marquart say about John Stormer's None Dare Call it Treason? ____.
5. *Agenda – Grinding America Down* shows ____.
6. Among those whose socialistic and anti-Communist views are exposed in *Agenda – Grinding America Down* are ____.

MARQUART'S WORKS

VOL. I
POPULAR WRITINGS

VOL. II
COMMUNISM

VOL. III
CHURCH AND MINISTRY

VOL. IV
APOLOGETICS

VOL. V
CHRISTENDOM

VOL. VI
JUSTIFICATION

VOL. VII
WORSHIP – LITURGY

VOL. VIII
BIBLE – HISTORICAL CRITICISM

VOL. IX
LUTHERANS

VOL. X
PERSON – (A TWENTY-FIRST CENTURY REFORMATION)

INDEX

140

141

BOOKS PUBLISHED BY LUTHERAN NEWS
www.christiannewsmo.com

A Burning and Shining Light, Paul Koch

A Handbook of Christian Matrimony, H. Otten

An American Translation of the Bible, William F. Beck

Baal or God, by Herman J. Otten

Bonhoeffer and King: Their Life and Theology Documented in Christian News, edited by Herman Otten

C.F.W. Walther's Pastoral Theology

Christian News Encyclopedia, Volumes 1-5

Crisis in Christendom Seminex Ablaze, Herman Otten

Devotions on the Apostles Creed, by Peter Krey

How To Start or Keep Your Own Missouri Synod Lutheran Church, J.M. Cascione

Islam In The Crucible, by R. da Montecroce and Martin Luther

Lil' Hillbilly coloring books (set of 4)

Luther Today, H. Otten

Luther's Small Catechism (AAT text)

Lutheranism from Wittenberg to the USA, Clement

Marquart's Legacy, Herman Otten

Marquart's Works, Vol. I

Pass the Salt, J.B. Romnes

Prayers for the Worship Service, Arthur J. Clement

Reclaiming the Gospel, How to Keep Your Congregation Lutheran, J. M. Cascione

Salt, Light and Signs of the Times, Ronald W. Stelzer

Servant Captains for the Good Ship Missouri

The Christ of the Gospels, W. F. Beck

The Christian's Travel Guide to World History, Henry Koch

The Lutheran Catechism on Homosexuality, Dr. David Kaufmann

The New Testament with Psalms & Proverbs in the Language of Today

The Wonders of Creation, Alfred Rehwinkel

Two Rivers to Freedom, Stella Wuerffel

Walter A. Maier Still Speaks - Missouri and the World Should Listen, Herman Otten